TO
GOD
Be The
GLORY

TO GOD Be The GLORY

USING SCRIPTURE TO OVERCOME
LIFE'S STRUGGLES

CHRISTENE McGEE

EDITED BY
KAREN REDLACK

Dedication

To my sons, DeVincent and Zion, there are no limits!! If you can think it, you can do it and become it. The only limitation is YOU. Keep God first, and He will give you the desires of your heart.

To my grandchildren, Madalynn, Ciara, Cayden, and Devan (and to all of my future grandchildren), I wrote this book for you. I wanted to record my experiences to remind you that no matter how low you may sink or how bad things may look—Trust God! When you can't depend on anyone, or you feel alone, left out, or any negative emotion that I wish I could protect you from—TRUST GOD! Your MiMi wholeheartedly trusts Him. He has never failed me, and He will never fail you! Always keep Him first, and He will protect and guide you.

Disclaimer

I am not a theologian, nor have I been to seminary school or been called to be an apostle, prophet, evangelist, pastor, or teacher of the Word of God (Ephesians 4:11). I am a believer that wants everything the Bible says that I'm supposed to have, and I want to do everything that the Bible says that I can do. I believe that Jesus died on the cross for my sins, rose in three days, and now sits at the right hand of God (Hebrews 10:12). I know that God is not a man that He should lie. He will never go back on His Word. If He said it, He'll do it, and if He spoke it, it will come to pass (Numbers 23:19). I believe that with all of my heart. This book is my testimony.

All scriptures are taken from the New International Version Bible (NIV) unless stated otherwise.

CONTENTS

INTRODUCTION

Life is so unpredictable. Knowing that I could trust the Lord has helped me to get through many things. My favorite verse of all time is Romans 8:28—and we know that all things work together for good to those who love God, to those who are called according to His purpose. To me, that means that whatever you are going through, if you believe and trust God, it is to your benefit. No matter how much of a setback you think it is, how much it hurts, how disappointed you are—it will work out in your favor when you trust the Lord.

For me, getting that verse deep down in my spirit made such a huge difference. I truly believed that if God allowed something negative to happen, there was a lesson for me to learn, it was for my protection, or had a purpose. Things that generally would ruin my whole day didn't upset me at all, knowing that Scripture.

Once while driving to work, I hit a pothole in the street and blew my tire out. I remember quoting that Scripture and looking down the road noticing that a stoplight was ahead. I found myself saying, "thank you, Jesus." I told myself, maybe it was for my protection. Who knows? Perhaps if I kept at that same speed, someone was going to run the light and hit me. Whether that's true or not, I don't know, but it felt better to think that rather than let it upset my day.

Using Scripture I have been able to get through many obstacles, heartbreaks, and long nights. I believe that Jesus set an example for us on how to act when in adverse situations. After being filled with the

Holy Spirit, He was led by the Spirit into the wilderness and tempted by the devil. Each time, Jesus responded to the devil with Scripture.

Matthew 4:1-11 says that the devil initially said for Him to command that these stones become bread. Jesus answered by saying, "It is written, man doesn't live by bread alone" (Deuteronomy 8:3). Then the devil took Him up into the holy city, set him on a pinnacle, saying, "if you are the Son of God, throw yourself down, for it is written, He will command His angels concerning you to guard you in all your ways; they will lift you up in their hands, so that you will not strike your foot against a stone" (Psalms 91:11-12). Let's stop right there and note that the devil knows the Bible! Now he's quoting Scripture. Again, Jesus answered, saying, "It is written, you shall not tempt the Lord your God" (Deuteronomy 6:16). Then the devil took Him up to an exceedingly high mountain showing Him all the kingdoms of the world and said, "All these things I will give you if you will fall down and worship me." Jesus said to him, "Away with you, Satan! It is written you shall worship the Lord your God and serve Him only" (Deuteronomy 6:13).

Modeling myself after Christ and quoting Scripture has helped me through some of the darkest nights. I've written this book giving my account of God's grace, mercy, love for His children, and faithfulness to His Word. The events in this book happened to me within 18 months. In John 4:39, after the Samaritan woman talked with Jesus, she went back into her town saying, "Come and see a man who told me all I've ever done." Scripture says that because of her testimony, many of them believed. My prayer is that by my testimony, many of you will find that the Word of God is alive, full of power, and that you will begin to seek and trust Him.

Chapter 1

TRAIN UP A CHILD

I was brought up in the church. As a child, I sat in church, passing notes to my cousin Kim. I was an usher, in the choir, went to every Vacation Bible School (VBS) during the summer, was in every Christmas and Easter program, and any other program a kid could be in at church. As a young adult, I stopped going to church, telling myself, "I had enough church as a child to last me a lifetime!" Don't get me wrong. I maintained my relationship with the Lord and believed in prayer.

What I found interesting was that after being out of the church about a year or two and returning, I still remembered Scriptures and stories from the Bible. Knowing this, as I raised my children and now have grandchildren, even when it seems they aren't listening in church, I know it is taking root. Start children off on the way they should go, and even when they are old they will not turn from it (Proverbs 22:6).

I always knew when trouble would arise that I could turn to the Lord. Eventually, I realized that I not only needed to go to Him in trouble, but I needed to praise Him and reach out to Him daily. After all, He promises DAILY BREAD (Matthew 6:11).

October 2016- I had numbness and weakness in my legs. While walking, my legs would give out, and I would catch myself from falling. Once coming down the stairs at my home, running to get something out of the oven, my legs gave out, and I hit the floor hard, later causing a large bruise to my right buttock. Not to alarm my husband who looked up, I got up, saying that I was okay and went on into the kitchen. I was concerned.

I went to see my doctor, who started with labs and did some motor reflex testing in her office. She said that we'd wait for the lab results and, if negative, do a CT scan or an MRI basically to rule out other things, including Multiple Sclerosis (MS). With 26 years of nursing experience, I was familiar with the symptoms that patients experience as MS progressed—muscle spasms, weakness, loss of coordination, balance problems, and sometimes cognitive decline, to name some common issues. I was stunned a little.

Before I could even get the lab results back, things grew worse fast. One day, I was downstairs and wanted to go up. I'm standing on the bottom step and couldn't get my legs to move. My brain works, so I'm thinking and saying for my legs to move, even using all of my strength, but my legs would not and could not step up! Eventually, I crawled up the stairs and grabbed hold of the railings, using my upper body strength, I pulled myself up to my feet.

At that point, I broke down, crying and calling out to God. I was home alone. I said every Scripture that I could remember. Jeremiah 1:12 says that God actively watches over His Word to perform or fulfill it. If God is watching over His Word, looking for someone with just a mustard seed of faith (Matthew 17:20), to take Him at his Word, here I am, Lord.

I reminded Him that He raised Lazarus from the dead, healed the lepers, made the blind to see, the deaf to hear, and the lame to walk. I added that He is the same yesterday, today, and forever (Hebrews

13:8). He is able to do exceedingly, abundantly, above all that I ask or think (Ephesians 3:20). Jesus bore all sickness and sin for us. Adding that by His stripes, I am healed (1 Peter 2:24). He Himself bore my sickness and iniquity (Isaiah 53:4-5).

Every Scripture that I could pull from memory, I did. Your Word says this, and Your Word says that! I remember saying you are the same God! You can heal me. This is Your will. The children of Israel wandered in the wilderness for 40 years, and Scripture says that there was not a feeble person among them (Psalm 105:37). You are able!

Something was awakened in me. I realize how bold I was to call God out at His Word. I was raised to believe you don't question God. I also knew that sickness and illness were not from God, but the enemy, the devil. The devil prowls around like a roaring lion looking for someone to devour (1 Peter 5:8).

I didn't know that's how God wants us to be—BOLD! Take Him at His Word. James 1:6 says ask boldly, believing, without a second thought. Hebrews 4:16 says, let us come boldly to the throne of grace. My favorite Scripture about boldness is a parable spoken by Jesus about a friend asking his neighbor for bread. It reads in Luke 11:8-9 that if friendship is not enough to make him get up to give you bread, your boldness will make him get up and give you whatever you need.

I tell you, go boldly, ask, believing that God is able, and you will be amazed. No eye has seen, no ear has heard, and no mind has conceived, the things God has prepared for those who love Him (1 Corinthians 2:9). That was over two years ago. I have not had any more weakness or numbness in my legs.

Chapter 2

FAST AND PRAY

January 1st, 2017—going into this new year after being healed and not having any more leg weakness, I made my New Year's resolution to read the Bible daily. After committing, it wasn't hard at all. My youngest son Zion walked in one day as I was reading and said, "Mom, you are reading and smiling like you are reading a best-selling novel." I laughed and said, "I am!" All of the years of feeling like I didn't understand some things I read in the Bible, it was crystal clear.

By March, I had learned more about fasting. The basic definition is simply abstaining from food for spiritual purposes. Fasting intensifies prayer. God always tells us to humble ourselves. James 4:10 says humble yourselves before the Lord, and He will lift you up. 1 Peter 5:6 says humble yourselves, therefore, under God's mighty hand that He may lift you up in due time. There are several other places in the Old Testament where we are told as well to humble ourselves.

2 Chronicles 7:14 says—If my people who are called by My name will humble themselves, and pray and seek My face, and turn from their wicked ways, then I will hear them from Heaven and will forgive their sin and heal their land. Well, how do we humble ourselves? In

Psalm 35:13 David says that he humbled himself (soul) with fasting. Daniel fasted until he heard from God (21 days). When the angel appeared, he told Daniel that since the day he humbled himself before God, his words were heard (Daniel 10:12).

All Scripture is God-breathed and is useful for teaching, rebuking, correcting and training in righteousness, so that the servant of God may be thoroughly equipped for ever good work (2 Timothy 3:16-17). As I continued to study Scripture, one thing I didn't do is to add to God's Word. He meant what He said, and He said what He meant.

Knowing this gives new meaning to Matthew 6. In verse 5, Jesus said when you pray, not if, which to me implies that as Christians, we are expected to pray. As Christians, I'm sure we can all agree on that. Keep reading. Matthew 6:16 says, moreover, when you fast... Again, implying to me that it is expected.

Jesus continues to say, when you fast, do not look somber as the hypocrites do, for they disfigure their faces to show others they are fasting. Truly I tell you, they have received their reward in full. Verse 17 says—but when you fast, put oil on your head and wash your face so that it will not be evident to others that you are fasting but only to your unseen Father; and your Father, who sees what is done in secret, will reward you openly.

Fasting was new to me. I was told years ago that you could give up something that was enjoyed, and it counted as fasting. Over the years, I've given up certain food items like chocolate and things like social media. I found in Scripture, everyone that fasted, gave up food for a period of time.

I decided to do a 3-day fast, water only. I didn't tell anyone in my home, not even my husband. As the Scripture said above, I wanted it to be between God and me. I still cooked dinner for my family every night.

Day 1

Today was a struggle, but whenever I felt hungry, I would quote Scriptures, read the Bible, or listen to a sermon on YouTube. That night I prayed myself to sleep. It felt great knowing I could control my flesh to commit to God.

Day 2

"Okay, I got this!" Believe it or not, I didn't feel hungry. That evening, Zion went for a jog. I was headed upstairs, so I locked the front door. Upon returning and finding the door locked, he started to bang on the glass of the door. Yeah, not smart. His arm went through the glass door, and when pulling his arm back out, he did significant damage. He severed an artery (yes blood was everywhere), cut through tendons, veins, and nerves.

I called out to Jesus first for help. Psalm 50:15 says call on me when you are in trouble, I will rescue you, and you will give me glory. I ran and grabbed a towel, looked frantically around for something to tie around his arm to slow the bleeding (feeling somewhat panicked to see blood shooting from his artery), and grabbed my phone to call 911.

While waiting for the ambulance to arrive, I continued to pray. My son was so calm, which was good. I had been an Intensive Care Unit (ICU) nurse for 22 years. If he had gotten excited, that would have sped his heart rate up and increased his blood loss. I remember saying, "devil, you are a liar!"

The ambulance arrived and took him to the closest hospital. Zion remained calm, joking, and at times, appeared to flirt with the nurses. I was amazed by the amount of blood loss, yet no loss of consciousness or feeling faint. This was a small hospital; he needed a vascular surgeon and had to be life-flighted to the Medical Center in Houston.

Zion was put into the helicopter, and I couldn't ride with him. I waited for my oldest son, DeVincent, to come to pick me up and take me to the medical center. I called to tell my husband, Vincent, what happened and he stated that he would head to the hospital. He was farther away than I was and driving an 18-wheeler. I knew that Zion would be taken immediately into surgery. As a mother, I began to feel scared for him that he would be rushed into surgery with no family there to reassure him. There's always traffic in Houston. I knew I wouldn't make it; I was still at least 20 minutes away.

While en route to the hospital, I made three additional phone calls. I called my friend Jacque Richards (may she now rest in Heaven), my friend Patricia Flowers, and my sister Brenda to pray. Jesus said if two of you on earth agree about anything they ask for, it shall be done for them by my Father in Heaven (Matthew 18:19).

It's a must to have some prayer warriors on your side. There is power in prayer of agreement! According to that Scripture above, you only need ONE person to agree with you. There is also strength in numbers. The Bible says one could chase a thousand, two put ten thousand to flight (Deuteronomy 32:30). By those odds, three can chase one hundred thousand and four a million! Within minutes of hanging up, Jacque sent me a message that she had added Zion to her prayer group from church. I felt a sense of relief because I know that prayer changes things!

Vincent called to say that he had made it and was able to see Zion before he went into surgery. I immediately began to cry and thank God. How did he make it so fast? He was farther away than I was. How did he find a place to park his truck and trailer? I realized at that moment that I was in the middle of a fast. Had the devil attacked my son because of this to discourage me? Probably so. Did it? No. I continued to fast and pray.

While Zion was in surgery, I went into the restroom and called on the Lord to be inside that operating room, guiding the surgeon's hands. It was around 9:00 PM when he went into surgery. Because nerves, veins, tendons, and arteries needed to be reattached, we were told he would be in surgery until possibly 4:00 AM. To our surprise, the surgeon came out around 12:40 AM, saying it was "clean-cut" and easily repaired. But God!

Day 3

Zion was discharged from the hospital. I continued to fast throughout the day and completed my final day of fasting. Throughout the fast, I quoted scriptures like Ephesians 3:20—He is able to do exceedingly, abundantly, above, all that I ask or think, according to the power that works in me. That is definitely my go to for ANY circumstance. Another scripture that kept me encouraged was—no weapon formed against me shall prosper (Isaiah 54:17).

Now, when I fast, I pray for a covering over my family before starting. I was surprised that after the first day I didn't feel famished. During that fast, I was reminded of how God tested Abraham. God told Abraham to take his only son Isaac up on a mountain to sacrifice him (Genesis 22). Abraham didn't have a lick of sense but to be obedient, trusting that if he killed his son, God could even raise the dead (Hebrew 11:19). What faith! How do you know you have faith if you are never placed in a situation to prove that you trust God?

My definition of faith is believing what God said He'd do, that He's done it, even when you don't have proof. Before Zion started therapy on his hand and wrist, I prayed about it, then started thanking God for a full recovery and full range of motion. I had no proof that he would have that. I just believed it and claimed it! Matthew 11:24 says, therefore, I tell you whatever you ask for in prayer, believe that you have received it, and it will be yours. I believe that is the key to answered prayer... believing without proof. If you already know the outcome, you don't need faith. The late R. W. Schambach said that most of us say, "I'll believe it, when I see it" but God says, "you will see it, when you believe it." All things are possible for one who believes (Mark 9:23).

Zion has since regained full range of motion to his left wrist, feeling in his fingers, and barely a noticeable scar, which was important for a then 17-year-old. The scar looks like a perfect number 7, which is the spiritual number for the Holy Spirit, completion, and perfection. Coincidence? I don't think so. He now has a permanent reminder of how great God is.

Chapter 3

POWER WITHIN ME

A hunger was born for me to have an even closer relationship with the Lord. I once read that theologians have said that there are 8,886 promises in the Bible, I wanted them all! For no matter how many promises God has made, they are "yes" in Christ. And so through Him the "Amen" is spoken by us to the glory of God (2 Corinthians 1:20). Amen actually means SO BE IT!!

There are nine gifts of the Spirit, and I wanted them all! Three vocal gifts—prophecy, speaking in tongues, and interpretation of tongues. Three revelation gifts—wisdom, knowledge, and distinguishing between spirits. Three power gifts—faith, healing, and miraculous powers. All are works of one Spirit and given to all (1Corinthians 12: 4-11). I speak on these gifts more in a later chapter.

Before leaving earth, Jesus told his disciples that the Spirit of truth, the comforter will come and guide you into truth (John 16:13). In Luke 11:13, He said, "if you then being evil, know how to give good gifts to your children, how much more will your heavenly Father give the Holy Spirit to those who ask Him."

I watched countless videos of R. W. Schambach on YouTube as he laid hands on people, and I often wished I had a church to go to where that could happen to me. I googled and attended a Church of God in Christ, and several Pentecostal churches searching to be filled with the Holy Spirit. Yes, now I know that sounds crazy.

All of my life, I have been taught about salvation. Yes, being saved is very important. It wasn't until I started studying God's Word for myself that I found out that He has promised us more than salvation! I didn't need to seek the Spirit. One day, I reread Luke 11:13—"if you then being evil, know how to give good gifts to your children, how much more will your heavenly Father give the Holy Spirit to those who ask Him." Could I just ask? I don't have to have hands laid on me? So I did just that, I asked to be filled with the Holy Spirit.

The late John Osteen was a great teacher of the Word. I listened to two to three sermons a day. I could relate to him because he talked about how he sought the Spirit. John also taught me about using the name of Jesus. He said in a sermon, that is the ONLY name the demons would respond to. In Luke 10:19, Jesus said, "behold I give you authority to trample on snakes and scorpions and to overcome all the power of the enemy, nothing will harm you." In John 14:12-13, Jesus said, "truly I tell you whoever believes in me will do the things I have been doing and they will do greater things because I am going to my Father. I will do whatever you ask in my name so that the Father may be glorified in the Son. You can ask me for anything in my name, and I will do it." God is such an on-time God. I did not realize that finding this out would help me very soon and that I would be exercising the authority to use Jesus' name.

The devil comes to steal, kill, and destroy. Jesus said, "I have come that you might have life and have it more abundantly" (John 10:10 King James Version (KJV). To me, an abundant life is MORE than enough. One thing I recognized immediately is that once I committed to reading my Bible daily, having frequent chats with God, and sought the Holy Spirit, the enemy was after me. I knew who was causing trouble. I was in a spiritual battle! Lucky for me, I knew that this battle was not mine, but God's (2 Chronicles 20:15) and greater is He that is in me, than he that is in the world (1 John 4:4). I needed only to resist the devil, and I knew that he would flee from me (James 4:7).

Ephesians 6:12 says, for our fight is not against flesh and blood but against principalities, against the rulers of the darkness of the world, and against spiritual forces of evil in the heavenly places. Though we walk in the flesh, we do not war according to the flesh. For the weapons of our warfare are not carnal, but mighty through God to the pulling down of strongholds (2 Corinthians 10:3-4).

About two months after Zion's accident, my husband was in an accident in his truck. He was fine, thank you, Jesus, but his work truck was totaled. During that time, we also received a letter from the Internal Revenue Service (IRS) saying we were being audited. Devil, you will not steal my joy! I have Scriptures committed to memory for every situation. My favorite for this financial storm was an oldie but goodie- no weapon formed against me shall prosper (Isaiah 54:17), followed by Deuteronomy 28:3 paraphrased—I am blessed in the city, blessed in the country, blessed coming in and going out, I am the top, not the bottom. I will lend and not borrow; my children are blessed.

I just decided to remain faithful in prayer, knowing that there is nothing too big for my God! I like to personalize and call Him mine. I also like to personalize Scripture. It wasn't my job to figure out how, I just began to thank Him that it was done. I went so far as to claim that, in the end, the IRS would owe us money. The Lord will fight for me, I only need to be still (Exodus 14:14). It is the Lord's battle to avenge and defend (Deuteronomy 32:35), not mine.

A few months after receiving notice from the IRS, we entered into hurricane season and had nonstop rain here in Houston, a.k.a. Hurricane Harvey. We had about 2 inches of water come into our home. We didn't have flood insurance because we didn't live in a flood zone. We applied for Federal Emergency Management Assistance

(FEMA) and we were denied. They had thousands of claims, and if you could still live in your home, you didn't qualify. I felt discouraged, but like David, I encouraged myself in the Lord (1 Samuel 30:6). I remembered thinking God is working this out in our favor. He will get glory from this. After all, had FEMA given us money, I would have credited our home repairs to them. God wants the glory!

We had family who wasn't able to help, but again I told myself, then they would be credited for helping to restore our home; God wants the glory. We lost two cars in that flood. In a matter of four months, we went from having four cars to only having one. That one car just happened to be the oldest out of the four. One day, coming home, it stalled at the light.

I felt overwhelmed. I got home and was led to read about Job. I looked at my situation and imagined God saying, "you can test her, but you can't kill her" as He said about Job (Job 1:12). I imagined this being a test to see if I would continue to praise the Lord, despite all of this happening to me. Though He slay me, yet will I trust in Him (Job 13:15 KJV).

After praying, I laid across my bed to read my Bible. I was overcome with emotion and began to cry. Honestly, I have never cried as easily as I cry now. There's something about when God takes out a stony heart and gives you a heart of flesh. I will give you a new heart and put a new spirit in you; I will remove from you your heart of stone and give you a heart of flesh (Ezekiel 36:26).

Just like that, I was overcome with joy! I found myself on my bed laughing hysterically. I laid there laughing, then began praising God. I later heard a sermon by the late Derek Prince. When asked if he remembered when he was filled with the Holy Spirit, he described being in his room, and after reading Scripture and praying, he was filled with uncontrollable laughter.

Job is the oldest book in the Bible. I believe that book was written as God's way of showing us what the devil is capable of. God has said,

I will never leave you nor forsake you (Hebrews 13:5). When you go through the waters, it will not overflow you and when you go through the fire, you will not get burned (Isaiah 43:2). Why? Because I am there! (Ezekiel 48:35). The Lord your God goes with you (Deuteronomy 31:6).

Don't give up, hang onto the horns of the altar. God is a restorer and wants our baskets (accounts) to overflow and for us to have the desires of our heart. I believe that the key to answered prayer is to continue to praise the Lord during your troubles. A little act of faith. It causes God to move and for the devil to flee.

Lessons learned from all of my experiences summed up to this, trust in the Lord. Lean not on your own understanding, in all your ways acknowledge Him, and He will direct your paths (Proverbs 3:5-6). God wants us to have unwavering faith, no matter how good things look or how bad it seems. There's nothing that you can go through that is too big for God to handle, so take your hands off! Be still and know that I am God (Psalms 46:10).

I was listening to a sermon and the minister was asked, how do you know that you've been filled with the Holy Spirit? He responded, "TROUBLE! The devil won't bother those who aren't a threat. That's why he's messing with you!" That made me smile. I'm proud to announce that the same Spirit that raised Jesus from the dead lives in me.

TO TITHE OR NOT TO TITHE

January 2018—I have now completed reading the Bible daily for an entire year. At this point, daily Bible reading is a habit. It's incredible what you will learn when you began to study God's Word for yourself. There are so many scriptures and stories of the Bible that I had never heard, and I've been in church most of my life. Like most, I received what the pastor fed me on Sunday and thought I was okay until the next Sunday.

Just like fasting was something new for me, paying my tithes consistently was also something new. Don't get me wrong; I always gave something in the church. What I gave would be considered an offering. I would give $5 or $10 into the offering plate as I walked around or as it was passed down the row. Tithing is different. Tithing is setting apart for God the first tenth of your income. Matter of fact tithe means 1/10 or 10%. Even over the years, when I considered myself to tithe, I realized I did it wrong. You give to God FIRST; people who wait to give after they receive or after they have paid all of the bills due, are not giving in faith.

There is a lot of controversy on whether you should or should not pay tithes—Old vs. New Testament. No, we are not under Old Testament law; we are under New Testament grace. For the law was given through Moses; grace and truth came through Jesus Christ (John 1:17). No doubt that has been established.

Here's what I know and believe—no matter what's read in the Bible or where, God will honor His Word. After all, 2 Timothy 3:16-17 says that all Scripture is God-breathed and is useful for teaching, rebuking, correcting, and training in righteousness, so that the servant of God may be thoroughly equipped for every good work.

My thoughts are this, if we are under the New Testament, a better covenant, shouldn't we be more generous? Some people go to church expecting lights on, heat in the winter, and air conditioning in the summer. How do you think the bills get paid? Your tithes. I feel that being able to give 10% back to God shows that He is important in my life, and that I'm concerned with the upkeep of His house.

Now before you stop reading, hear me out. I ran into scriptures that I had never heard before I began to study God's Word for myself. I want to share those scriptures with you and let you know that I, for the first time, committed to paying my tithes and have been financially blessed! I feel that I am doing you an injustice if I don't mention this, and sadly many in the pulpit are failing us because they do not want to be considered a "prosperity preacher." Psalm 35:27 says that the Lord takes pleasure in the prosperity of His children. Their job is to tell us "what thus said the Lord," and that's what I plan to do while giving you my testimony.

Malachi 3:8-10 "Will a man rob God? Yet you rob me. But you ask, 'how are we robbing you?' "In tithes and offerings. You are under a curse- your whole nation because you are robbing me. Bring the whole tithe into the storehouse, that there may be food in My house. Test Me in this," says the LORD Almighty, "and see if I will not throw open the floodgates of Heaven and pour out so much blessing that there will not be room enough to store it. I will prevent pests from devouring your crops, and the vines in your field will not drop their fruit before it is ripe," says the LORD Almighty. Just. Wow. My favorite part of that Scripture is "test Me in this."

Haggai 1:6 "You have planted much, but harvested little. You eat, but never have enough. You drink, but never have your fill. You put on clothes, but are not warm. You earn wages only to put them in a purse with holes in it." Haggai 1:9 says, You expected much, but it turned out to be little. What you brought home, I blew away. Why? Declares the LORD Almighty. Because of My house, which remains a ruin, while each of you is busy with your own house". This verse reminds me of all of the times I worked overtime only for an unexpected repair or something to come up. I never got to enjoy that extra money.

To be clear, once Jesus walked the earth, conquered the grave, and rose again, He left us with a new commandment. Romans 6:4 clearly states that we are not under law (the commandments by Moses) but grace. The New Testament speaks more about helping the needy and being a generous giver. Acts 20:35, Jesus said, "it is more blessed to give than to receive."

The only times that Jesus mentioned tithing was in a parable comparing a Pharisee with a tax collector in Luke 18: 9-14 and in Matthew 23:23. In Matthew, paraphrased, He said "woe to you, teachers of the law and Pharisees, you hypocrites! You give a tenth, but neglect more important matters like justice, mercy, and faithfulness. You should have practiced the latter without neglecting the former." Hmmm, I'm no Bible scholar, but it clearly says not to neglect to tithe.

2 Corinthians 9:6-7 reminds us that whoever sows sparingly will reap sparingly, and whoever sows generously will reap generously. Don't be reluctant or under compulsion, for God loves a cheerful giver. Give and it will be given to you. A good measure, pressed down, shaken together and running over, will be poured into your lap. For the measure you use, it will be measured to you (Luke 6:38).

I know what you may be thinking because I thought the same thing. How do I know what the pastor is doing with my money? For all I know, he may be buying drugs or doing God knows what! Rest assured, God knows! That's not your concern. Your concern is to be obedient to God's Word. Your next thought, "I can't afford to tithe; I'm behind on most of my bills." My response, you can't afford NOT to tithe. Have faith that God is not going to have you evicted because you are obedient to His Word. Lack of faith? Get in His Word. Faith comes by hearing, and hearing comes by the Word of God (Romans 10:17). You need faith because, without it, it is IMPOSSIBLE to please God. You need to know first that He is, and secondly, that He is a rewarder of those who diligently seek Him (Hebrews 11:6).

Despite the setbacks, IRS notices, totaled vehicles, and a damaged home needing repairs, I continued to pay my tithes and fully trusted God's Word, knowing that blessings would come. Have an expectancy attitude! I continued to plant my seeds weekly. I knew that my season and harvest would come. God is always on time.

Things started to look up financially. My car is a 2009 and paid for. I started talking about it being time for me to get a new car. I found a job that provided me a rental car that only rents the latest model cars. Look at God! Paul said it best when he said, "And my God will meet all your needs according to His riches in Christ Jesus" (Philippians 4:19).

I have received a few unexpected checks in the mail, credits to my accounts, and getting estimates that were a lot lower than I expected to pay. Repairs have been made in our home with upgrades. Things that I have wanted for years, have been done. All of these things are paid in full. I'm not bragging. I'm very grateful and give ALL glory to God! I'm mentioning this to you only to emphasize the "Test Me in this" part of the Scripture from Malachi that I referenced earlier.

If you have all of the money that you need, great, continue to do what you are doing. If you are living paycheck to paycheck, I don't care what your grandmother or mother has done in the past, especially if all they have known is a struggle. Test God for yourself. Give it six months and prepare for Him to amaze you. Make God a priority with everything that you do, especially with your finances, and He will supply all of your needs and will give you the desires of your heart.

I remember when I started paying my tithes consistently, as soon as I paid it, I expected a breakthrough right away. Trust God. Keep planting those seeds. He is an amazing God. Let us not become weary in doing good, for at the proper time we will reap a harvest if we do not give up (Galatians 6:9). I kept planting and planting, not knowing that He would harvest an abundance that I wasn't expecting. He has blessed me so that I can now be a blessing to others. He has exceeded my expectations!

But seek first His kingdom and His righteousness, and all these things will be given to you as well (Matthew 6:33). God knows what we need before we ask (Matthew 6:8). For I know the plans I have for you, declares the LORD, "plans to prosper you and not to harm you, plans to give you hope and a future" (Jeremiah 29:11).

Chapter 5

TASTE AND SEE

As soon as I felt that things were starting to look up, a new dilemma presented itself. One day, Zion came to me and said that he had lost his sense of smell and taste. He has always suffered from his allergies. He was started on some allergy medication and a nasal spray. About a month later, he came showing me that there was a protrusion on his forehead. I felt it, expecting it to feel soft, but it felt hard like bone.

He went in to see our family doctor who put him on antibiotics and sent him for an x-ray. Two days later, our doctor sent him for a CT scan because the x-ray was inconclusive. Four hours later, I received a call from his doctor saying that he was placing him on more potent antibiotics. Zion appears to have a tumor (mass) that has eaten through bone, and he is at risk of meningitis, and he needs to see a specialist ASAP. Devil, you are a liar!

After His resurrection, Jesus returned to His disciples, and He said—"And these signs will follow those who believe: in my name, they will drive out demons, they will speak in new tongues; they will pick up snakes with their hands; and when they drink deadly poison, it will not hurt them at all; they will place their hands on the sick, and they will get well" (Mark 16:17).

In John 14:12, Jesus says, "very truly I tell you, whoever believes in me will do the works that I have been doing, and they will do even greater things than these because I am going to the Father. And I will do whatever you ask in My name, so that the Father may be glorified in the Son. You may ask me for anything in My name, and I will do it." Sidenote- that is why we end all of our prayers in Jesus' name.

I understood more about the Holy Spirit, so where is the power? I don't see many preachers in the pulpit exercising this power the Bible speaks of. I'm really glad that I sought this on my own without having someone misguide me or give me false information. Get in God's Word for yourself! He will open the scriptures to you. I've read the Bible from front to back about three times now and each time, I see something new. I've found that a lot of times when I'm reading the Bible, the Bible is reading me!

Back to the scripture—it says any BELIEVER could do this. I continued to look deeper, meditate on Scripture, and ask God to reveal things to me. I became hungrier. I wanted to know more and to experience more. Acts 1:8 says that you will receive power after the Holy Ghost has come upon you. Those scriptures didn't say I needed to run to my pastor, or that only the head of the church could do these things. It said any BELIEVER had this power. I know that Jesus walked this earth for 30 years and never performed a miracle until the Holy Ghost descended on Him as a dove (Luke 3:22).

Is anyone among you sick? Let them call the elders of the church to pray over them and anoint them with oil in the name of the Lord. And the prayer offered in faith will make the sick person well; the Lord will raise them up. If they have sinned, they will be forgiven (James 5:14-15).

I called my son into the room. I asked him, "do you believe that Jesus is the same yesterday, today, and forever? That what He did years ago He can do today?" My son answered, "yes, I believe that." I told him that I have some Holy Oil that has been prayed over by others in agreement with our prayers. I'm going to anoint my hands, and we are going to pray for this growth to disappear in the name of Jesus. I know what you're thinking, and the answer is, NO. I've never done this before. There's something about when Scripture gets so embedded, and all doubt is removed. You truly believe His Word, knowing that God's Words cannot fail or return void as stated in Isaiah 55:11.

I anointed my hands and placed my right hand over the growth on Zion's forehead. We prayed for that growth to shrivel up and die and for his sense of smell and taste to return. I never pray without citing Scripture, not that God needs to be reminded, but I'm letting Him know, I'm holding on to THIS promise. I ended the prayer by letting God know that He will be given all the praise, all the honor, and all the glory. In Jesus' name. Amen.

Hebrews 11:1—Now faith is confidence in what we hope for and assurance about what we do not see. Basically, believing what you desire or have asked God for is done, even when you don't see it or have proof that your prayer was heard. Just believe. Looking at my son, the growth still protruded from his forehead. I took it by faith, telling Zion, just watch God. He cannot lie nor fail to fulfill His promises (Numbers 23:19). My son said, "Mama, I know. When you touched it, I felt warmth."

The next day Zion walked in with Wingstop. He came into my room and said, "you may not believe this, but for the first time in months, I can taste and smell again! I just tore those lemon pepper wings up!" I smiled and said, "won't He do it!" We still went to see the specialist who gave him another round of antibiotics and a steroid. The protrusion disappeared without further intervention.

I'm crediting this to the Lord, not medicine. He has yet to fail me. He wants us to take Him at his Word, without doubt, and to know that He is able and willing. Taste and see that the Lord is good; blessed is the man who trusts in Him (Psalms 34:8).

BE ANXIOUS FOR NOTHING

With so much going on in the world, it's easy to see why some people have an anxiety disorder or major depression. Anxiety is nervousness and fear of the future. What ifs. Most depression stems from the past. Should haves, could haves, and would haves. Either way, it pulls us away from the present. Worry. Worry. Worry. By giving it to God and taking your hands off, it allows God to move on your behalf. I heard a minister on YouTube (I forgot his name, or I'd give him credit) say that as long as your hands are on it, God's hands are off of it and cannot move.

I believe that we need to pray about it then start praising God as if it is done. Of course, with no evidence that your prayers have even been heard, let alone answered! As I stated earlier, I believe God allows some things to test our faith. After all, how do you know that you have faith if it's never tested and applied?

One night, I'm half asleep in bed when I roll over to my side. I remember feeling tenderness to my right breast as I laid there. I felt underneath my right breast but wasn't lying on anything. I rolled onto my back and began to feel along the side of my breast. I sat straight up!

Nothing wakes you up like feeling tenderness and a lump in your breast. Honestly, I simply said, "fix it, Jesus," and I rolled over and went back to sleep. I'd be lying if I said I never thought of it again. I did. The next day I decided to do a full breast self-exam. Yeah, there it is around the 10 o'clock position.

I went for a mammogram, then an ultrasound, which confirmed there was a lump. An ultrasound-guided biopsy was ordered. I didn't fast when a tumor was found in Zion's sinuses, but I felt pulled to fast this time. Twenty-four years of marriage and my husband and I had never fasted together. I asked him to fast with me for two days before the biopsy. He did.

On the morning of the biopsy, we stood in the kitchen, holding hands, and prayed together. I remember smiling while driving to the mammography clinic, thinking that my marriage was as strong as ever. We were now connecting Spiritually as well. Sad to say, but I don't remember too many times standing together in prayer before leaving for work or leaving period. It felt good.

While waiting in my hospital gown, I started to feel anxious. I often tell people that I use the best anxiolytic ever—Scripture and prayer! I began to pray. Every time I had a negative thought, I had Scripture to combat it. Devil, you are a liar!

I remember thinking of when Jesus called Lazarus from the grave. The first key part happened before he even made it to the grave. He stated (paraphrased) that this sickness will not end in death. It is for God's glory so that the Son may be glorified (John 11:4). Now that's a God kind of faith! Speaking things into existence. Jesus is the best and only person that we should model ourselves after, so I said, "this biopsy will be done, it will be negative, and God will get the glory." To further calm myself, I cited 2 Timothy 1:7—God did not give us a Spirit of fear, but of power, love, and a sound mind. This anxiety was not a Spirit from the Lord. I rebuked it in the name of Jesus!
What do you do after you pray? PRAISE HIM. Praise Him like you

already know the results. Like you already have the biopsy results, and it hasn't even been done yet. Do you want to feel God's presence, or do you wonder where God is? Psalms 22:3 says He inhabits the praises of His people. Thank Him with no evidence.

Before getting on the table, I asked to go to the restroom. I prayed, "Father, I thank You, that You have heard my prayer. I know that there is nothing that You can't do! Your Word says ask and you will receive, seek and you will find, knock and the door will be opened to you (Matthew 7:7). I thank You that I can always stand on Your Word, and it will never fail me. I thank you in advance for this negative biopsy result. I will give you all of the glory. In Jesus' name. Amen."

This might seem weird. Two years ago, it would've been strange to me as well. There's something about when Scripture takes root, when you consecrate yourself (set yourself apart for use by God), and ask to be filled with the Holy Spirit.

I had no anxiety. Before starting, the doctor was explaining things about the procedure and how I'd get the results. Without hesitation, I said, "it's going to be negative." She said, "I sure hope so." I smiled and said, "it will." Wow, when did my faith get to this point? No evidence, but claiming it! While the biopsy was being done, I just kept saying to myself, "Thank you, Jesus. Thank you, Jesus."

God wants us to call those things that aren't as though they were (Romans 4:17). After all, we do have the power of life or death in our tongue (Proverbs 18:21). Let the weak say that I am strong (Joel 3:10). Always remember that the prayer of a righteous person is powerful and effective (James 5:16).

I was getting off from work one day when an unknown number called. I answered. It was the doctor calling to say the biopsy was negative. I said, "thank you; I knew it would be." She said, "yeah, I remember you saying that." Of course, I hung up and began to praise the Lord. His grace is sufficient, and His power is made perfect in weakness (2 Corinthians 12:9). His mercy is everlasting (Psalm

100:5).

Lastly, Philippians 4:6-7 says—do not be anxious about anything, but in every situation, by prayer and petition, with thanksgiving, present your requests to God. And the peace of God, which transcends all understanding, will guard your hearts and your minds in Christ Jesus.

FOR BETTER OR FOR WORSE

Scripture says that the devil goes around like a roaring lion, seeking whom he may devour (1 Peter 5:8), so we need to stay alert. The devil will try everything to discourage you, to cause you to doubt the Lord, in hopes that you will say, "before I became so committed to the Lord, I didn't have these troubles," and turn away. I'm writing my testimony to let you know, DON'T give up. The devil is only after you because you are a threat, and he knows that God is about to elevate you and to use you. Many are the afflictions of the righteous, BUT the Lord delivers him out of them ALL (Psalms 34:19) (Emphasis mine).

When the devil tempted Jesus, and He resisted, the devil left him. Luke 4:13 says he left Him for a more opportune time. I used to read the Bible as stories, things that happened back in the day, now I realize that most were placed in the Bible as an example of how we should handle adversities. In my life, I'm starting to see a trend—my son's health, my health, our home, our vehicles, and our finances. The devil is busy, but I know he's after me because I'm a threat.

The devil wants nothing more than to destroy your marriage.

Marriage is the first covenant that God established with Adam and Eve, before even establishing the church. A covenant is a binding commitment. Marriage is a picture of the relationship between God and the church. The Bible also ends with a marriage. Revelations 19:7-9 says that Christ is coming back for His bride.

In the previous chapter, I just mentioned how my husband and I fasted and prayed together before my breast biopsy. That was about five weeks ago. Now we have disagreed and are walking through the house where the tension is so thick, and we are barely speaking. Devil, you are a liar!

Did I mention that this is happening a few weeks before our 25th wedding anniversary? No marriage is perfect; we have had our ups and downs for sure. This was extreme for us because the disagreement wasn't that serious, really a misunderstanding. I recognized who the trouble maker was and that this was spiritual warfare. Your brother, sister, neighbor, coworkers, husband or wife is not the problem. Recognize what's going on and rebuke that spirit! There is only one name and one name only that demons will respond to, and that is the name of Jesus! He has given us the authority to use His name.

In Luke 10:19, Jesus says, "I have given you authority to trample on snakes and scorpions and to overcome all the power of the enemy; nothing will harm you." We have to learn to use our God-given authority and stop letting the devil have his way! "I rebuke you in the name of Jesus! Get out of my house, off of my kids, off of my finances, out of my marriage, and out of my life!" James 4:7 says to resist the devil, and he will flee from you. The problem is, as the devil did with Jesus, he leaves only to come back at an opportune time to start something new. Keep resisting; eventually, the devil will leave you alone and go on to someone else.

I can't tell you how important it is to get into God's Word, no matter what you are going through. Get into His Word and find scriptures about your situation and hold on to them. I promise you, there is a scripture for your situation. For this time in my life, I remember reading and quoting, "he that finds a wife, finds a good thing, and obtains favor with the Lord (Proverbs 18:22). What God has joined together, let no man separate (Mark 10:9). Love is patient; love is kind. It does not envy; it does not boast; it is not proud. It does not dishonor others; it is not self-seeking; it is not easily angered; it keeps no record of wrongs. Love does not delight in evil but rejoices with the truth. It always protects, always trusts, always hopes, always perseveres. Love never fails (1 Corinthians 13:4-8).

If God allows you to be tested, He will get you through it. Once you are through it, your marriage, finances, health, etc., will be stronger than ever. Why do we have to go through things? I don't know, but as I said in the introduction, all things work in your favor when you love the Lord. Sometimes I simply say, "God I don't understand, but I trust You. Give me the grace to deal with this". He will! Grace is undeserved favor. It can't be earned or bought. You just have to believe/receive it by faith.

The Bible says that a house divided against itself cannot stand (Matthew 12: 25). That means that a husband and wife in disagreement will not be able to withstand internal and external pressures and will fall/fail. As husband and wife, we should be in agreement and on one accord. We are one flesh. Genesis 2:24 says, therefore, a man shall leave his mother and his father and hold fast to his wife, and they shall become one flesh. So they are no longer two but one flesh (Mark 10:8).

Communication, prayer, and keeping God first are crucial for a successful marriage. We've all heard that a family that prays together stays together. It's true. Keep others out of your marriage. You said your vows before God and your covenant is with Him. It should be God, you, and your spouse. Ecclesiastes 4:12 says that one may be overpowered, two can defend themselves, but a cord of three strands is not quickly broken. By keeping God as center of your marriage, He will guide, direct, and His love will keep you two bound. God is the glue that holds a marriage together.

Men are responsible for provision (1 Timothy 5:8) and protection. Ephesians 5:22-33 sums up marriage comparing Christ and the church. Verse 22 starts by saying for wives to be submissive to their own husband... I always laugh that God needed to clarify whose husband you need to submit to... YOUR OWN. It goes on to say that the husband is the head. Decisions and direction come from the head. I didn't say this, God ordained it this way. We are told to be submissive, but ladies relax, the bulk of the responsibility lies with men. We should submit to our husband as to the Lord. For the husband is head of the wife, as Christ is head of the church. As the church submits to Christ, so also wives should submit to the husband in everything (v 24). A husband should love a wife as his own body. He who loves his wife, loves himself, and the wife must respect her husband (v 33).

Husbands should love their wife as Christ loved the church and gave Himself for it. This is not a taking love, but a giving love. With God as center, you will be amazed at how your bond will grow. There is a transparency, honesty, loyalty, and an acceptance. Amos 3:3 asks "can two walk together unless they be in agreement?" We need to be in harmony with our spouse. Pray for each other.

Let's take it back for a minute. In the beginning, God said, let us make mankind in our image, in our likeness. So God created mankind in His own image, in the image of God He created them, male and female He created them (Genesis 1:26-27). God took the dust from the ground and formed a man. He then breathed into his nostrils the breath of life, and the man became a living being (Genesis 2:7).

If we are made in His image and scripture says in multiple places that He loves to be praised (Psalm 150:6, Psalm 100:4, Jeremiah 20:13 to name a few), and that He is a jealous God (Exodus 20:5, Exodus 34:14, Deuteronomy 6:15, Isaiah 42:8), that applies to us as well. We are made in His image! We all want praise, a compliment, and thank you every now and then.

In Genesis 2:18 God said, "it is not good for man to be alone. I will make a helper suitable for him." God caused Adam to fall into a deep sleep, removed a rib, then God made woman from the rib he had taken out of the man. The man said, "this is now bone of my bones and flesh of my flesh: she shall be called 'woman' for she was taken out of man." That is why a man leaves his father and mother and is united with his wife, and they become one flesh. When you get married, your old life dies, and you become one.

I believe the purpose of the wife, as stated above is to help. To honor, uphold, and encourage. To me, a helper is not inferior. The Holy Spirit was called a "helper" by Jesus (John 15:26). Be faithful to the job assigned to you. Husbands are to treat their wife with respect as the weaker partner and as heirs with you of the gracious gift of life, so that nothing will hinder your prayers (1 Peter 3:7).

The order is as follows- God, Christ, man, then woman. The head of every man is Christ, and the head of the woman is man, and the head of Christ is God (I Corinthians 11:3). Ladies, as hard as it may be sometimes, we have to allow them to make decisions. In most marriages, women tend to take the lead and/or provision away from men. I'm guilty. God had a specific purpose for men and women when we were created.

After I started this closer walk with God, He subtly reminded me of some things done in the past when I had gone against decisions that my husband had made that I didn't agree with. I was taking the head away from him. I repented because that was not scriptural for me to do that.

We serve such an awesome God! He has a way to convict us without condemning. If you ever feel condemned and full of guilt, it's not from the Lord. His approach is so gentle that you are like "yea, I was wrong", but not to the point of constantly thinking about it or feeling guilt. That's the enemy's strategy. There is no condemnation for those who are in Christ Jesus (Romans 8:1). For God did not send His Son into the world to condemn the world, but to save the world through Him (John 3:17).

If you are married to a man that has not accepted his role, pray for him. If you aren't sure where the breakdown is in your marriage, you should ask God to show you where the problem is, He will show you. If you have feelings of "I did this" or "this is because of what I've done in the past"- shake that spirit off of you. All have sinned and fallen short of the glory of God, and all are justified freely by His grace through the redemption that came by Jesus Christ (Romans 3:23). Once you have repented and asked for forgiveness, God throws your sin in the depths of the seas, (Micah 7:19), to be remembered no more. He has forgotten it, let it go. Your slate has been wiped clean.

If you are single, or previously married and divorced, be specific with your prayers. I specifically prayed for a God-fearing man years ago when in reality I don't even think I truly knew what that meant. It is not a fear like being afraid or feeling like you're falling off of a mountain or going to be attacked by a lion, it's a fear of high regard. An awe or reverence, to think highly of and not want to displease the Lord. Love for God is the motivation, not fear. The fear of the Lord is the beginning of wisdom (Proverbs 9:10). A married couple should submit to one another in the fear of God (Ephesians 5:21).

We live in a world where there are temptations, let's be honest. The devil is busy as I've said numerous times. The fear of the Lord will keep you faithful and help you to honor your vows before God, because you know that God is everywhere (omnipresent) Psalm 33:13-14, knows everything (omniscient) 1 John 3:20, has unlimited power (omnipotent) Colossians 1:16, and never sleeps nor slumbers (Psalm 121:4)!

Paul said in scripture, if you want to know how successful a man is, look at his wife. Is she cared for physically, emotionally, socially and all of her needs met? I Corinthians 11:7 says that a woman is the glory of man. So men, your wife is your glory. Your wife is an extension of you. Your wife reflects the level of care and attention that you give her. Sorry fellas, but if your wife is mean and always mad, check yourself and what's going on in your house.

I've heard a lot of women say they strive to be a Proverbs 31 woman. She is a wife of noble character, worth more than rubies. Her husband has full confidence in her and lacks nothing of value. She brings him good, not harm all the days of her life. She sets about her work vigorously. Extends her hands to the needy. Her husband is respected. She is clothed with strength and dignity and can laugh at the days to come. She speaks with wisdom. Her children arise and call her blessed, her husband also, and he praises her. A woman who fears the Lord should be praised.

Things I've learned in 26 years of marriage.

1. I think the most important thing is to keep God first. Go to church and worship together. Early in our marriage when we had marital problems, my husband's late grandfather, Daddy Joe, just bluntly asked one day when we were at his house—"where do y'all go to church?" At that time, we weren't in church regularly, so we told him that. He basically told us that was our problem, and when we go back to Houston to find us a church. We did and it made a huge difference in our relationship.

2. Keep others out of your business. You may be surprised to know, some people want your marriage to fail for different reasons. Take your problems to the Lord and you won't have to worry about being gossiped about or making up with your spouse and now others seeing them differently.

3. Be each other's number one supporter and fan. Support the other's interests, ask questions, listen. Most marriages break up because an outside person comes in showing an interest not

shown at home. I should add, if you can't make a phone call, send a text, or an email in front of your spouse, then it probably shouldn't be done. Your spouse should be the first person you call if you have good news and the first person you call when you have bad news. Communication is crucial.

4. Keep the romance alive, go on dates and vacation. We try to vacate at least twice a year. Years ago, we couldn't afford to go to Costa Rico or Jamaica, we'd take a weekend getaway up the highway to San Antonio, Dallas, or somewhere drivable. The change of scenery does wonders.

5. Lastly, watch what you say in anger. Words hurt and can't be taken back, even after you've apologized, the sting is still there. We should be quick to listen, slow to speak, and slow to become angry. Human anger does not produce the righteousness that God desires (James 1:19). But now you must put them all away: anger, wrath, malice, slander, and obscene talk from your mouth (Colossians 3:8). The tongue has the power of life and death (Proverbs 18:21). Our tongues can tear others down or be used to build others up. I know it's a struggle, and my ace in the hole scripture when all else fails... I simply ask God to bridle my tongue! Set a guard over my mouth LORD; keep watch at the door of my lips (Psalms 141:3).

As I've said before, once you get through the trial, you will be stronger. The devil remains busy, but with God as head of the home, there will be an unbreakable bond.

Chapter 8

SPIRITUAL WARFARE

I listened to a sermon by R. W. Schambach (I'm sure you can tell by now how much I love to listen to him), and he had the congregation turn to their neighbor and say, "I have more power than the devil." He added, "be careful, he will be outside waiting for you! You have to eyeball that devil and stand your ground!"

The devil is an evil spirit and he has many minions (demons) working for him. Jesus calls him our adversary (1 Peter 5:8). He wants to kill you and your loved ones, affect your health, your children's health, your finances, your marriage, etc. He comes to steal, to kill, and to destroy, but Jesus said, "I have come that you may have life, and have it more abundantly (John 10:10).

The gospel according to John highlights the Father and Son relationship. God is Spirit (John 4:24). In John 1:1 Amplified Bible (AMP), it says, In the beginning [before all time] was the Word (Christ), and the Word was with God, and the Word was God Himself. He was [continually existing] in the beginning [co-eternally] with God. All things were made and came into existence through Him; and without Him not even one thing has been made that has come into being. The Word became flesh, and made His dwelling among us (John 1:14). Jesus says in John 10:30, "I and my Father are one" and He says in John 14:9, "Anyone who has seen Me has seen the Father."

When Jesus walked the earth, He regularly freed those with evil spirits. So from those scriptures alone, we know that evil spirits can enter a human body and cause you to do evil things and/or control you. In Mark 5:9, there was a man living among the tombs (graveyard) cutting himself and separated from society. Jesus cast the evil spirits out saying, "come out of this man, you impure spirit". Mark 5:15 says, the man that had been possessed by the demons was sitting there dressed and in his right mind.

When Jesus came down from the Mount of Transfiguration, a father approached and knelt before Him saying that his son was suffering. His son has seizures and often falls into the fire or into water. Jesus rebuked the demon, and it came out of the boy (Matthew 17:14-18). And also some women who had been cured of evil spirits and diseases: Mary (called Magdalene) from whom seven demons had come out (Luke 8:2).

Today in the world, there is so much hatred, school shootings, racial tensions, etc. I believe it all stems from Satan's plan and people being possessed by evil spirits. Jesus called him the ruler of this world and the father of lies (John 8:44). For we wrestle not against flesh and blood, but against principalities, against powers, against the rulers of the darkness of this age, against the spiritual hosts of wickedness in the heavenly places. Therefore, take up the whole armor of God that you may be able to withstand in the evil day and having done all, to stand (Ephesians 6:12-13).

Luckily for us as Christians, we know who comes out victorious in the end. As we saw with Job, the devil can only do what God allows. Why does God allow it? That I don't know. What I've found is that He has given us the means to fight back—THE NAME OF JESUS.

I also know that we are surrounded by so many doubters and

unbelievers! In Genesis 1:26 (KJV), God gave man dominion over all the earth and over every creeping thing that creepeth upon the earth. God honors the choices made by man. We are not puppets or robots. He is not going to make us worship, love, or believe His Word. Psalm 115:16 says the heaven, even the heavens are the LORD's; but the earth He has given to the children of men. God did say this- If My people who are called by My name will humble themselves and pray and seek My face and turn from their wicked ways, then I will hear from heaven, and I will forgive their sin and will heal their land (2 Chronicles 7:14).

I once talked to someone whose sister had been diagnosed with cancer. She felt that God did that to her sister to humble her. God does not cause these things. We have to stop blaming God. God is love. Whoever does not love does not know God, because God is love (1 John 4:8). He wants us well, healthy, happy, prosperous, lacking nothing (James 1:9). God is no more going to give someone cancer to humble them than you would throw your child into the street to teach him/her about traffic or place their hand on fire to teach them it is hot!

God loves us and wants the best for us! Hosea 4:6 says- my people are destroyed for lack of knowledge. God has given us power over the enemy yet some of us are still waiting on God and He is waiting on us. I was the same way. I believed that Jesus died on the cross, and I believed that He was coming back again, but I lacked faith for now. Jesus is alive.

Paul wrote to the Ephesians saying—Finally, be strong in the Lord and in His mighty power. Put on the full armor of God, so that you can take your stand against the devil's schemes. For our struggle is not against flesh and blood, but against the rulers, against the authorities, against the powers of this dark world and against the spiritual forces of evil in the heavenly realms. Therefore, put on the full armor of God, so that when the day of evil comes, you may be able to stand your ground, and after you have done everything, to stand. Stand firm with the belt of TRUTH around your waist, with the breastplate of RIGHTOUSNESS in place, and your feet fitted with the readiness that comes from the gospel of PEACE. In addition to all of this, take up the shield of FAITH, with which you will be able to extinguish all of the flaming arrows of the evil one. Take the helmet of SALVATION, and the sword of the SPIRIT, which is the WORD OF GOD (Ephesians 6:10-17). (Emphasis mine).

This is spiritual warfare. Note that your sword is the Word of God. The weapons we fight with are not the weapons of the world, but they have divine power to demolish strongholds. (2 Corinthians 10:4). Use the Word to God as your weapon! Say what God says about situations.

My oldest son DeVincent was asleep in his room and called me on the phone around 2:00 AM. When I answered he simply said, "Mama come to my room!" I went into his room to find him twisted up in bed with his head hyperextended and turned into the pillow. He had color changes to his face which implied that his airway was compromised (oxygen was restricted).

I asked, "what's wrong, can you turn over?" he cried saying that he couldn't. He explained that he had felt for his phone in the dark and had called me without looking at his phone. His neck was rigid, with distended veins, and his body was tensed. He said, "feels like something is holding me down, I can't breathe".

Is this an evil spirit holding him down? Had I ever rebuked an evil spirit before? NO! The Bible warns that an evil spirit returns bringing seven other spirits worse than itself (Matthew 12: 43-45). I called out for Jesus. Then you will call, and the Lord will answer; You will cry, and He will say "here I am" (Isaiah 58:9). There are still lots of things that I don't know, I just have faith in God's Word and stand on it. Having said that, I don't think this should be done unless you have full faith in God and in what you are doing.

I went and anointed my hands with Holy Oil, then began to touch my son and pray, rebuking any and everything, in Jesus' name! I could feel his tense body relax. His clenched jaw relaxed. His distended veins in his neck relax. The color in his face returned.

I realized I was becoming the type of Christian God wants us to be. Taking the shield of faith to combat all of the flaming arrows of the devil. When Jesus died and was resurrected on the third day, He conquered the enemy! Jesus is the only name that they will run from!

R. W. Schambach was laying hands on people and putting oil on them. He says that someone asked him "where did he get the Holy Oil, is it from the Holy Land?" He replied, "no this is my wife's cooking oil!" His point was that it's not the oil, it is the FAITH that's behind the oil. Years ago, I had never touched Holy Oil, now here I am using it on my other son.

As long as I have breath in my body, I will keep my family covered! How long will we continue to sit back while our homes are destroyed, and our kids are addicted to drugs and our marriages fail. If you lack faith to do some of the things that I'm stating in this book, I urge you to get into God's Word. Faith comes by hearing and hearing from the Word of God (Romans 10:17). I don't think it's possible to get into scripture every day and not be changed and not have your faith in Christ increased. For without faith, it is impossible to please Him, for he who comes to God must believe that He is (real), and that He is a rewarder of those who diligently seek Him (Hebrews 11:6). Search the Scriptures, the answers are there. Jeremiah 29:13-14 says "you will seek Me and find Me when you seek Me with all of your heart. I will be found by you," declares the LORD.

That was a year ago. My son has not had any other incidents like that, and I have faith in God that he won't ever again! Matter of fact, a couple of weeks after this, my son called me on a Saturday night asking me if I was going to church the next day. I said "yes" and he responded that he was going with me. This was a first, him asking me, normally it's the other way around.

When it was time for alter call, he stood up! He gave his life to the Lord. Tears of joy flowed down my cheeks. As for me and my house we will serve the Lord (Joshua 24:15). I love what the Pastor said next, "The moment you stood up, the angels rejoiced, and God wiped your slate clean!"

The devil has been after my oldest son for a while, but I refuse to give up. Don't you! As children of God, we need to be intercessors and pray and petition God on behalf of nonbelievers (Isaiah 59:16). We should speak life and salvation over our children! Hang on to these Scriptures and personalize them! Deuteronomy 28:4—My children will be blessed. Psalm 112:2—My children will be mighty in the land. Acts 16:31—Believe in the Lord Jesus, and you will be saved, you and your household. No doubt the enemy will come again from another angle, but I am well equipped!

Chapter 9

DISCERN MUCH?

I wanted all that a child of God was entitled to have. Please note that my faith didn't increase overnight for me to do what was mentioned in previous chapters. I became hungry for God's Word. I no longer listened to the radio while driving but only to the Bible on audible or a sermon from YouTube. I not only went to church on Sundays, like I've done for years, but I went to Bible study on Tuesday night and Wednesday night service. I could not get enough of God's Word!

Faith comes by hearing and hearing from the Word of God (Romans 10:17). Increasing my knowledge in God's Word increased my faith to lay hands on my sons. I don't suggest you do this without developing a stronger relationship with God first, otherwise you may find yourself like the seven sons of Sceva, a Jewish chief priest. They were attempting to cast out demons and the evil spirit answered them saying, "Jesus I know, and Paul I know about, but who are you?" Then the man with the evil spirit jumped on them and overpowered them all. He gave them such a beating that they ran out of the house naked and bleeding (Acts 19:13-16). Jesus also warned that an evil spirit may return bringing with himself seven other spirits more wicked than himself, and they go in and live there, making the final condition of the person worse than before (Matthew 12:45).

There's something else I had to do to increase my faith and that was to turn off the TV and social media. An idol is something that you worship. I believe whatever you think about the most, especially first thing in the morning and the last thing you think about before you fall asleep, you probably idolize. Sadly, for me, it was Facebook. As soon as my eyes opened, I grabbed my phone to get on Facebook. In bed I was on Facebook until my eyes got heavy and I fell asleep. I realized that I spent hours a day on Facebook/social media. Time that took me away from God. I changed that! God wants to be first. He has said- "You shall have no other gods before me" (Exodus 20:3), "for you should not bow down to them or worship them; for I, the LORD your God, am a jealous God" (v 5).

For some people, it's another person, for example a boyfriend or girlfriend, it can be money, success, cars, etc. Whatever you give the most thought to, especially when waking up and falling asleep you probably are idolizing. We should not love anything or anyone more than we love God. He wants and longs for our undivided attention.

For me to get to this level of faith, I deactivated my social media. When I wake up now, I pray and read my Bible. Before bed, I pray and read my Bible. It actually started to seem like I had a better day and slept better!

My sister Marie would always say over the years that the Holy Spirit told her something. I longed for that more than ever. To hear and be directed by the Spirit. One day I had a craving for a Subway sandwich. I haven't had Subway in probably over a year. When I called to tell my husband I was stopping there after work, to see if he wanted anything, he was like "I didn't know you liked Subway." I then called my son Zion to say the same, and he was like "Subway??"
I went on into Subway, and as I was placing my order, I could hear a baby in the back. As I moved on toward the register, I saw an infant in

a car seat. I asked about the baby and the young man nodded towards a female stocking the chips.

I left and got to my car and I had this strong sense to give her $40. I sat there wondering where did that come from? I simply prayed, "God if this is You telling me to do this, You have to give me the words." I'm a generous person to family, but can't say I have felt this urge before towards a stranger. I immediately recognized it was a prompting by the Holy Spirit.

My bank's ATM was right across the parking lot. I drove over there to get $40 but requested $60 instead. I mean if $40 is a blessing than $60 is better. I was reminded to be obedient! God promises DAILY bread (Matthew 6:11, Luke 11:3). So I stuck the other $20 in my purse. I drove back across the parking lot to Subway, thinking, what am I gonna say? As clear as day I heard, "tell her Jesus loves her."

I went back into Subway. The young man looked up puzzled as if my order was wrong. I told him I wanted to speak to the young lady. She came out and standing in the hallway alone, I said, "I was just in here. I see your baby is back there." She said, "yeah my babysitter canceled, but I need to work." Handing her the money I said, "I want to give you this, and tell you that Jesus loves you." She looked at that money and doubled over crying. She thanked me saying that she needed gas and diapers and had been praying. I commended her for bringing her child with her, it shows her determination to make things better for them.

I went back to my car and cried. God had used me as a vessel! As I drove away, I was reminded 30 years ago, as a single mom, when I drove to work on fumes and a lady had given me $30. It was like she had given me $300. I had forgotten about that! Because I was at work at a nursing home and not supposed to take money from family members, I told her "no, I can't accept that" as BAD as I needed it! The woman stuck the money into my scrub top and said, "God told me to give that to you, and I'm not gonna let you cause me to miss my blessing!" and she walked away. Like the young lady that I had just blessed... I had been praying. That was my first incident of being prompted by the Spirit, I believe you would call that a message or word of knowledge because how did I know she needed gas and diapers without the Holy Spirit guiding me.

John 14:15—Jesus speaking said, "If you love me, keep my commands. And I will ask the Father and He will give you another advocate to help you and be with you forever—the Spirit of truth. The world cannot accept Him, because it neither sees Him, nor knows Him but you know of Him. But you will know Him, for He lives with you and will be in you." John 14:26—But the Advocate, the Holy Spirit, whom the Father will send in My name, will teach you all things and will remind you of everything I have said to you.

There are different kinds of gifts, but the same Spirit distributes them. There are different kinds of service, but the same Lord. There are different kinds of working, but in all of them, and in everyone, it is the same God at work. Now to each one the manifestation of the Spirit is given for the common good. To one, there is giving through the Spirit, a message of WISDOM, to another a message of KNOWLEDGE by means of the same Spirit, to another FAITH by the same Spirit, to another gifts of HEALING by that one Spirit, to another MIRACULOUS POWERS, to another PROPHECY, to another DISTINGUISHING BETWEEN SPIRITS, to another SPEAKING IN DIFFERENT KINDS OF TONGUES, and still to another INTERPRETATION OF TONGUES. All these are the work of one in the same Spirit and He distributes them to each one just as He determines. Just as a body, though one has many parts, but all its many parts form one body, so it is with Christ (1 Corinthians 12:4-12). (Emphasis mine).

In summation, there are nine gifts of the Spirit-

- 3 vocal gifts (prophecy, speaking in tongues, and interpretation of tongues)
- 3 revelation gifts (wisdom, knowledge, and distinguishing [discerning] between spirits)
- 3 power gifts (faith, healing, and miraculous powers)

Paul said we should desire gifts of the Spirit especially prophecy (I Corinthians 14:1). I desired them ALL. I acknowledge that I have the gift of faith because the things I've mentioned in the previous chapters couldn't be done unless you have a supernatural faith boost. A God kind of faith.

I realized that God would show or tell me things in a dream, most times a word of wisdom or word of knowledge. I know it sounds crazy, but I left my last job after I had a dream. Best decision I've ever made! Honestly, I don't know how I've lived almost 50 years without the Holy Spirit directing me!

Discernment is the ability to judge well, notice details, and recognize. I think I have always had discernment, and the ability to recognize that someone or something is not right. That feeling of "I don't know what it is, but there's something about her." I believe that discerning of spirits is different. It is it is a supernatural gift which enables you to know the source of spirits, whether demonic, from the Holy Spirit, or the human spirit; things not known by natural senses but the inner motivations of the heart.

For the Word of God is living and active, and sharper than any two edged sword, piercing to the division of soul and of spirit, joints and of marrow, and discerning the thoughts and intentions of the heart (Hebrews 4:12). Beloved do not believe every spirit, but test the spirits to see whether they are from God, for many false prophets have gone out into the world (1 John 4:1).

I must tell you that when God starts to manifest gifts, it can be frightening. Some things you'd rather not know. Hence that cliche that ignorance is bliss! God has shown me so many things! People who have a spirit of jealousy or lying have been revealed to me. The Spirit showed me this. I would have never suspected any of this.

This is a supernatural gift! He will start to reveal things to you that you could only know supernaturally. I will add this, when God exposes a person and shows you who they really are—BELIEVE IT! My prayer is for me to know and use the information appropriately. Why was this revealed to me? Probably for my protection. What am I to do with this information? Sometimes that's the hard question. I've already realized that everything revealed to me is not to be shared. Don't waste what is holy on people who are unholy. Don't throw your pearls to pigs! They will trample the pearls, then turn and attack you (Matthew 7:6 New Living Translation (NLT). Basically, they won't appreciate it and may attack you for it.

One day, I was out shopping in the town where I grew up, and I ran into a female I hadn't seen in over 20 years. I had my beautiful granddaughters with me, Madalynn and Ciara. After exchanging hellos, she immediately brought up an abusive relationship that I was in when I was younger. I've been with my husband now for 29 years and we've been married 26 at the writing of this book.

I'm sure I looked at her with a surprised look on my face. I mean, that's the first thing you want to talk about? The Holy Spirit showed me she had an evil spirit. Matter of fact, when I looked her in the eyes, her eyes would shift back-and-forth. I simply told her "I'm grateful the Lord sent me my husband who wouldn't dare lay a finger on me!" She actually continued to talk about an incident that happened when I was with that abusive person, that I don't even remember! I smiled and said "Girl let it go! I have." Devil, you are a liar. You are not going to ruin my day and take me back to that space.

Because I could sense an evil within her, the conversation was over. I simply left her with a "God bless you" to which she didn't reply.

WHO DOES THAT?! Satan! His whole strategy is guilt. He loves to bring up the past and remind you of things. "I remember when you used to..." Let it go sis! I'm only concerned with pleasing the Lord. I've repented and He has thrown it all into the sea of forgetfulness to be remembered NO MORE (Hebrews 8:12). (Emphasis mine).

No doubt, someone who knew the old Christene will read this book and say, "I remember when she used to..." or when "she used to date so and so..." Let it go! Don't carry around MY BURDENS that I'm not even carrying. We have to learn to say what God says about us.

Here are a few for you to get down in your spirit DAILY.

- **I am forgiven.** If we confess our sins, He is faithful and just to forgive us our sins and to cleanse us from all unrighteousness (1 John 1:9 New King James Version (NKJV).

- **I am blessed.** Behold, I have received a command to bless. He has blessed, and I cannot reverse it (Numbers 23:20). And God is able to bless you abundantly, so that in all things, at all times, having all that you need, you will abound in every good work (2 Corinthians 9:8).

- **I am made new.** Therefore, if anyone is in Christ, he is a new creation; old things have passed away; behold all things have become new (2 Corinthians 5:17).

- **I am saved!** If you confess with your mouth the Lord Jesus and believe in your heart that God has raised Him from the dead, you will be saved. For with the heart one believes unto righteousness and with the mouth confession is made unto salvation (Romans 10:9-10). For whoever calls on the name of the Lord shall be saved (Romans 10:13).

- **I am delivered.** For He has rescued us from the dominion of darkness and brought us into the kingdom of the Son He loves, in whom we have redemption, the forgiveness of sins (Colossians 1:12-13). And it shall come to pass that whosoever shall call on the name of the LORD, shall be delivered: for in Mount Zion and in Jerusalem shall be deliverance, as the Lord has said, and in the remnant whom the Lord shall call (Joel 2:32 KJV).

- **I am redeemed.** Christ redeemed us from the curse of the law by becoming a curse for us, for it is written: "Cursed is everyone who hung on a pole." He redeemed us in order that the blessing given to Abraham might come to the Gentiles through Christ Jesus, so that by faith we might receive the promise of the Spirit (Galatians 3:13-14). In Him we have redemption through His blood, the forgiveness of sins, in accordance with the riches of God's grace (Ephesians 1:7).

- **I am well and healthy.** I will fulfill all my days on this earth. Be not wise in your own eyes, fear the Lord and turn away from evil. It will be healing to your flesh and refreshment to your bones (Proverbs 3:7-8). Do you not know that your body is a temple of the Holy Spirit within you, whom you have from God? You are not your own, for you are bought with a price. Therefore, honor God with your body (1 Corinthians 6:19-20). Lastly, I will live and not die and proclaim the works of the Lord (Psalms 118:17)!

- **I am justified.** Since we have now been justified by His blood, how much more shall we be saved from God's wrath through Him (Romans 5:9). For it is not those who hear the law who are righteous in God's sight, but it is those who obey the law who will be declared righteous (justified) (Romans 2:13). Finally, Romans 4:25 says He was delivered over to death for our sins and was raised to life for our justification. I love the definition that the late Derek Prince gives for the word justified. He says justified means "just as if I'd never sinned."

I'm praying that other gifts will manifest in me with guidance of how to use each gift. People can tell when you've changed, they don't call to gossip about others marriages, children, etc. They recognize that I'm not the same person to listen to such trash. I'm happy about that. In place of that I've noticed that people will call me to pray with them or call me for me to be in agreement with prayer for family, friends, and situations. I'm happy about that.

Honestly when people see me, I don't want them to see Christene, I want them to see Jesus. It is a daily struggle. I am far from perfect, nor do I pretend to be perfect. Everyday I have to ask God to take the lead, and for me to be obedient and pleasing to Him. Luke 9:23- then Jesus said to them, "if anyone desires to come after Me, let him deny himself, and take up his cross daily, and follow Me."

I am such a sinner and know that only a sinner needs a savior! Lucky for me, Christ Jesus came into the world to save sinners (1 Timothy 1:15). The Lord knows I take up my cross daily!! As Paul said, I have been crucified with Christ. It is no longer I who live, but Christ who lives in me. And the life I now live in the flesh I live by faith in the Son of God, who loved me and gave Himself for me (Galatians 2:20).

Chapter 10

DREAMS DREAMS

My point throughout this book, that I hope is not missed, is that you have to get in agreement with what God says, that's the key. You don't need to run to your pastor or anyone else. You have a direct relationship with the Father. Commit Scripture to memory that you can pull from your heart during long, dark nights. THE SPOKEN WORD OF GOD IS YOUR SWORD (Ephesian 6:17). Model yourself after Jesus when in adverse situations, "IT IS WRITTEN" (Matthew 4:4, 7, 10). Speak His Word like a two edged sword (Hebrews 4:12), used aggressively and defensively, to keep the devil off of you! No, in all these things we are more than conquerors through Him who loved us (Romans 8:37). More than a conqueror means to come out of the battle with more than you went in with!

You are a believer, you pray, you have faith, the Spirit guides, and directs. There's something else that I've experienced- seeing dark shadows throughout my home and having frightening dreams. I started having what some may consider nightmares. I continued to pray my way through. Before bed I started reading Psalms 91 in its entirety. It's a prayer for protection that the devil knows well.

Remember the devil quoted Psalm 91:12 when he was tempting Jesus.

Once I was home alone and I saw dark shadows moving through my hallway. My heart started racing and I went and closed my bedroom door. Then I realized that I wasn't going to let this devil have me in fear, so I opened my door and said, "in the name of Jesus, leave my house and never return!" I know this sounds crazy, even to me as I write this. As embarrassing as some of these stories may be, I know without a doubt that others have experienced these things and my prayer is that my testimony will help others.

Years ago, my family and friends were raving about this movie called the War Room with Priscilla Shirer. After months of hearing about it, I finally watched it. In that movie she did a lot of what I'm saying to do in this book. What's amazing is that so many people have watched and loved that movie, but have yet to go through their home and do the things that she did, like opening her front door and casting evil spirits out!

I've never been a dreamer. I started having dreams all the time. It wasn't hard for me to distinguish between the fleshly "self" dream, spiritual dream, or a demonic dream. I just had to base it on how I felt. If I felt scared, panicked, uneasy, guilt, or deceived, and the room was dark, I knew it was from the devil. I could distinguish a fleshly dream by realizing that this was something that I thought about during the day or something that's going on in my life. A Spiritual dream would be full of color, full of light, and I would feel very peaceful, calm, and in a place of joy. If you are unsure of the source of your dreams, ask God. Genesis 40:8 says that interpretations belong to God.

I've always been afraid of spiders. I've almost had a wreck before, because I saw a tiny spider on my sun visor! The devil knows your fears and he will magnify your fears if you allow. I had a dream that I was looking at a spider go across the countertop, then it went down the drain into the sink. As I looked over into the sink, the spider was held up over my head and dropped on me. It was so real that I actually woke up, jumped out of bed, panicked, and started pulling my covers back looking for it. Then I realized how I felt panic and fear; this is a demonic attack. "You got me this time, but next time you won't," I remember thinking.

A few weeks later in my sleep, I was laying down on my side. Something runs toward me then jumped over me. It comes back from behind, jumps over me then runs away. It was dark. I sat up thinking "what was that?" and looking in the distance. An ugly, demonic, gargoyle looking being was face-to-face with me! My heart raced. All I could hear at that moment was R. W. Schambach saying, "you have to eyeball that devil!" So I did. I looked this demon right in the eyes and said "my elder brother whipped you over 2,000 years ago, get the hell out of my my house, out of my dreams, and out of my life! In Jesus' name!" Poof! He was gone. I just applied scripture to my situation. In Matthew 12: 50, Jesus said, "For whoever does the will of my Father in heaven is my brother and sister and mother."

Ephesians 6 says to put on the whole armor of God. If you visualize the protection given in the Scripture you will find that there is protection for your head, chest, body, and feet, but no protection to cover the back. We are not to run from the enemy but run towards him and place him in a defeated position which is under our feet. The God of peace will soon crush Satan under your feet. The grace of our Lord Jesus be with you (Romans 16:20).

Jesus said, "All authority in heaven and on earth has been given to Me" (Matthew 28:18). I have given you authority to trample on snakes and scorpions and to overcome all the power of the enemy, nothing will harm you. However, do not rejoice that the spirits submit to you, but rejoice that your names are written in Heaven (Luke 10:19-20).

If you suffer with insomnia and/or nightmares here are few additional scriptures:

Proverbs 3:24-26 says when you lie down you will not be afraid. When you lie down, your sleep will be sweet. Have no fear of a sudden disaster or of the ruin that overtakes the wicked, for the LORD will be at your side and will keep your foot from being snared.

Matthew 11:28, Jesus says, "Come to Me, all you who are weary and burdened, and I will give you rest. Take My yoke upon you and learn from Me, for I am gentle and humble in heart, and you will find rest for your souls. For My yoke is easy and My burden is light."

Psalm 23:4—Even though I walk through the darkest valley, I will fear no evil, for You are with me; Your rod and Your staff they comfort me.

Psalm 127:2—Unless the LORD builds the house, the builders labor in vain. Unless the LORD watches over the city, the guards stay and watch in vain. In vain you rise early and stay up late, toiling for food to eat—for He grants sleep to those He loves. I love KJV for that verse, it says He giveth His beloved sleep. There's no need to stay up worrying. Pray and go to sleep, thanking the Lord that your prayer has been answered.

One last thing that has happened in my sleep that I want to mention. One night, I was asleep and I heard my oldest son, DeVincent yell, "Mama!!" I sat up, asking "what is it? No one was there. The house was dark. My son has his own apartment now, why is he here yelling for me? And in the middle of the night. I looked over at my husband sleeping soundly, he didn't even seem to hear him. I got out of bed and went into the hallway, no one was there. I went into Zion's room, he was asleep. I went downstairs, it was dark, no one was there. That's weird.

I called DeVincent on the phone, but he didn't answer. I immediately got on my knees and started praying. The Holy Spirit knows whatever is going on with him and I was awakened because prayer was probably needed. I prayed and called out to God for his protection. I found out days later that at that moment, he needed someone to intercede on his behalf in prayer. Thank you, Jesus, for the prompting by the Holy Spirit.

Job 33:14-18 says, For God does speak- now one way, now another-though no one perceives it. In a dream, in a vision of the night, when deep sleep falls on people as they slumber in their beds, He may speak in their ears and terrify them with warnings, to turn them from wrongdoing and keep them from pride, to preserve them from the pit, their lives from perishing by the sword.

I've had so many dreams, good spiritual dreams. This book would never end if I attempted to write about all of them. God has shown me things, warned me about things, and people in my dreams. He is such an awesome God.

I actually attended a Prophetic and Spiritual Dreams conference for two days to help me to decipher my dreams. A Prophetess that was there actually told me that God was about to use me. That wasn't a surprise to hear because every day I ask Him to use me. To place me in situations where I can be a blessing to someone. I like how it's said in Isaiah 6:8—Then I heard the voice of the Lord saying, "Whom shall I send? And who will go for us?" And I said, "Here am I. Send me!"

The prophet Joel said, "And afterward, I will pour out my Spirit on all people. Your sons and daughters will prophesy, your old men will dream dreams, your younger men will see visions. Even all my servants, both men and women, I will pour out my Spirit in those days." (Joel 2:28-29). Resist the devil and he will flee from you (James 4:7). I no longer have nightmares, only peaceful sleep.

Psalm 91 (For Protection)

[1] Whoever dwells in the shelter of the Most High
will rest in the shadow of the Almighty.
[2] I will say of the Lord, "He is my refuge and my fortress,
my God, in whom I trust."
[3] Surely He will save you
from the fowler's snare
and from the deadly pestilence.
[4] He will cover you with His feathers,
and under His wings you will find refuge;
His faithfulness will be your shield and rampart.
[5] You will not fear the terror of night,
nor the arrow that flies by day,
[6] nor the pestilence that stalks in the darkness,
nor the plague that destroys at midday.
[7] A thousand may fall at your side,
ten thousand at your right hand,
but it will not come near you.
[8] You will only observe with your eyes
and see the punishment of the wicked.
[9] If you say, "The Lord is my refuge,"
and you make the Most High your dwelling,
[10] no harm will overtake you,
no disaster will come near your tent.
[11] For He will command His angels concerning you
to guard you in all your ways;
[12] they will lift you up in their hands,
so that you will not strike your foot against a stone.
[13] You will tread on the lion and the cobra;
you will trample the great lion and the serpent.
[14] "Because he loves me," says the Lord, "I will rescue him;
I will protect him, for he acknowledges my name.
[15] He will call on me, and I will answer him;
I will be with him in trouble,
I will deliver him and honor him.
[16] With long life I will satisfy him
and show him my salvation.

Psalm 23

A psalm of David.

[1] The Lord is my shepherd, I lack nothing.

[2] He makes me lie down in green pastures,

He leads me beside quiet waters,

[3] He refreshes my soul.

He guides me along the right paths

for His name's sake.

[4] Even though I walk

through the darkest valley,

I will fear no evil,

for You are with me;

Your rod and Your staff,

they comfort me.

[5] You prepare a table before me

in the presence of my enemies.

You anoint my head with oil;

my cup overflows.

[6] Surely your goodness and love will follow me

all the days of my life,

and I will dwell in the house of the Lord

forever.

Chapter 11

UNANSWERED PRAYERS

For verily I say unto you, that whosoever shall say unto this mountain, be thou removed, and be thou cast into the sea; and shall not doubt in his heart, but shall believe that those things which he saith shall come to pass; he shall have whatsoever he saith. Therefore, I say unto you, what things so ever you desire, when you pray, believe that you receive them, and you shall have them. And when you stand praying, forgive, if you have ought against any: That your Father also which is in heaven may forgive you your trespasses. But if you do not forgive, neither will your Father which is in heaven forgive your trespasses (Mark 11: 23-26 KJV). (Emphasis mine).

Jesus said, "when you pray, believe you have received it, and it will be yours", but goes on to say, when you pray if you hold anything against anyone, forgive them so that your Father in heaven may forgive you your sins. What if I told you that unforgiveness may be what's hindering your prayers being answered?

When I started my spiritual journey, I ran across that verse. I had people I needed to forgive. After all, I want my prayers answered and my sins forgiven! I had to crucify that old man "self." People that I had disagreements with, I called. Sometimes I honestly didn't know why we stopped talking. Funny thing, one person in particular, we couldn't even remember what happened! As embarassing as that is to admit, it is a perfect example of how the devil wants us to be! Isolated, angry, feeling unloved, anxious, and depressed. Any negative emotion that you may feel did not come from God. He gives us a Spirit of power, of love, and of sound mind (2 Timothy 1:7 KJV).

Some of us have brothers and sisters that we no longer talk to. I get it. I'm saying that may be hindering your prayers from being answered. Whoever claims to love God yet hates a brother or sister is a liar. But whoever does not love their brother and sister, whom they have seen, cannot love God, whom they have not seen (1 John 4:20). Forgive them. Even if you don't want to call them, pray about it and forgive them. God knows the heart. Truly forgive them and let that hurt go.

I think another hindrance to unanswered prayer is judging others. Do not judge, or you too will be judged. For in the same way you judge others, you will be judged, and with the measure you use, it will be measured to you. Why do you look at the speck of sawdust in your brother's eye and pay no attention to the plank in your own eye? How can you say to your brother, "Let me take the speck out of your eye," when all the time there is a plank in your own eye? You hypocrite, first take the plank out of your own eye, and then you will see clearly to remove the speck from your brother's eye (Matthew 7: 1-5). I think that is self-explanatory.

Another popular scripture about judging can be found in John 8:3-11. The teachers of the law and the Pharisees brought in a woman caught in adultery. They made her stand before the group and said to Jesus, "Teacher this woman was caught in adultery. In the Law of Moses commanded us to stone such women. Now what do you say?" They were using this question as a trap, in order to have a basis for accusing Him. But Jesus bent down and started to write on the ground with his finger. When they kept on questioning Him, He straightened up and said to them, "Let any one of you who is without sin be the first to throw a stone at her." Again He stooped down and wrote on the ground. At this, those who heard began to go away one at a time, the older ones first, until only Jesus was left, with the woman still standing there. Jesus straightened up and asked, "Woman where are they? Has no one condemned you?" "No one, Sir," she said. "Then neither do I condemn you," Jesus declared. "Go now and leave your life of sin."

First off, I've always found this passage very interesting. The accusers brought her in saying that she was caught in adultery. Correct me if I'm wrong, but there had to be another person involved, so why wasn't he brought in as well? Anyway, you get the point, stop judging others or you will be judged. Jesus is the only judge. For in the same way you judge others, you will be judged, and with the measure you use, it will be measured to you. (Matthew 7:2). He said in John 5:22, "Moreover, the Father judges no one, but has entrusted all judgement to the Son." For all have sinned and fallen short of the glory of God (Romans 3:23).

Here's a few additional things that may be hindering your prayers being answered:

- ***Check your life***. God is not going to bless you to live for the devil. So, you must ask yourself "Am I living right?" What I'm saying is, I don't believe it's God's will to bless you, so you can do something that displeases and doesn't give Him glory. For example, asking God to bless you financially so that you can do something illegal or against your marriage vows. That's not His will. The only way to know the will of God is through His Word. When I was younger, I'd pray "if it's Your will." Now I know better. I know His will and I stand on that promise. Matthew 6:10, part of the Lord's Prayer says, Your kingdom come, Your will be done, on earth as it is in heaven.

- ***Check what you are saying***. Are you praying for a healing then making it null and void by saying negative things. "I'm never gonna get better." Say what God says about you! I am well. I am healthy. I will live and not die. I will fulfill my days and proclaim the works of the Lord! (Psalm 118:17). The tongue has the power of life and death, and those who love it will eat its fruit (Proverbs 18:21).

• ***Check your faith***. The only way that I know to increase faith is by hearing God's Word and reading God's Word. So now faith, comes by hearing and hearing by the Word of God (Romans 10:17). And without faith it is impossible to please God, because anyone who comes to Him must believe that He exists and that He rewards those who earnestly seek Him (Hebrews 11:6).

• ***Check your praise***. After you have prayed... PRAISE HIM! Praise Him like you just received the title to your car, even though you are behind a payment. Praise confuses the enemy. The enemy knows how much money you have in your bank account, how confusing for you to laugh and thank Jesus when you see your bank statement. Scripture says to call those things which are not as though they were (Romans 4:17). Let the weak say, "I am strong!" (Joel 3:10).

• ***Check your prayer***. What if God didn't move until you prayed? Let's not wait until the end of the day. Be prayerful throughout the day. Every time my husband or children are leaving the house, I pray for protection over them until I see them again. I pray for my own safety. I pray for peace of mind. I pray for restful sleep. For He gives His beloved sleep (Psalm 127:2). I pray for my grandbabies getting on or off the bus for school. This list is continuous, because I'm always praying.

I like how David progressed in his praying and praise. In Psalm 55:17 David said—"Evening, and morning, and at noon, will I pray, and cry aloud; and He shall hear my voice" (KJV). Then in Psalm 119:164—it says Seven times a day I praise You for Your righteous laws, but in Psalm 34:1, David said, "I will praise the Lord at all times: His praise shall continually be in my mouth." (Emphasis mine).

Teaching the people from a boat, Jesus told them this parable: "A farmer went out to sow his seed. As he was scattering the seed, some fell along the path, and the birds came and ate it up. Some fell on rocky places, where it did not have much soil. It sprang up quickly, because the soil was shallow. But when the sun came up, the plants were scorched, and they withered because they had no root. Other seed fell among thorns, which grew up and choked the plants. Still other seed fell on good soil, where it produced a crop—a hundred, sixty, or thirty times what was sown. Whoever has ears, let them hear (Matthew 13:1-9).

Jesus goes on later to explain the parable. When anyone hears the message about the Kingdom and does not understand it, the evil one comes and snatches away what was sown in their heart. This is the seed sown along the path. The seed falling on rocky ground refers to someone who hears the word and at once receives it with joy. But since they have no root, they last only a short time. When trouble or persecution comes because of the word, they quickly fall away. The seed falling along the thorns refers to someone who hears the word, but the worries of this life and the deceitfulness of wealth choke the word, making it unfruitful. But the seed falling on good soil refers to someone who hears the word and understands it. This is the one who produces a crop yielding a hundred, sixty, or thirty times what was sown (Matthew 13:19-23).

Be the sower on good soil! Stand on God's promises, claim them, and don't let the enemy steal that or any promise from you! As the old folks used to say, He may not come when you want Him, but He's always on time! Be patient. But those who trust in the Lord will find new strength. They will soar high on wings like Eagles. They will run and not grow weary. They will walk and not faint (Isaiah 40:31).

Chapter 12

JESUS PAID IT ALL

I love how God has opened the Scriptures up to me revealing even the most intimate things. I will now take a Scripture and read it in different translations with concordance to really understand. It's a work in progress, but I want to fully understand God's Word. These last two chapters are so weighty, but so important. I did not feel qualified to try and explain this, but I kept feeling the pull to add these chapters, and knew I needed to be obedient. Romans 8:30 says that He also called those He had already appointed, He also justified those He called, and He gave glory to those He justified.

If there is anything in this book that is unclear to you, I am the best and only person to ask! I know what I meant, especially if something doesn't come across clear—ASK ME! I've decided, if there's something I don't understand in the Bible I need to ask God. All Scripture is God breathed and is useful for teaching, rebuking, correcting and training in righteousness, so that the servant of God may be thoroughly equipped for every good work (2 Timothy 3:16-17). God simply used the apostles and prophets to write through them via the Holy Spirit. Jesus Christ clearly confirmed this when speaking in Matthew 22:31.

He quoted Exodus 3:6 saying, "But concerning the resurrection of the dead, have you not read what was spoken to you by God, saying I am the God of Abraham, the God of Isaac, and the God of Jacob. God is not the God of the dead, but of the living." (Emphasis mine). Those are Moses' words. Jesus implies this is God speaking.

Many people have tried to disprove the Bible. The Bible was written years and even centuries apart. Yet the scriptures overlap and is told by different people, but it all falls perfectly into place. One thing I never do is argue scripture with anyone. There's no need to defend God's Word. His Word will stand on its own! Non-believers won't understand things of the Spirit.

As believers, "What we have received is not the spirit of the world, but the Spirit who is from God, so that we may understand what God has freely given us. This is what we speak, not in words taught us by human wisdom, but in words taught by the Spirit, explaining spiritual realities with Spirit—taught words. The person without the Spirit does not accept the things that come from the Spirit of God, but considers them foolishness, and cannot understand them because they are discerned only through the Spirit" (1 Corinthians 2:13-14).

Concerning the salvation, the prophets, who spoke of the grace that was to come to you, searched intently and with the greatest care, trying to find out the time and circumstances to which the Spirit of Christ in them was pointing when he predicted the sufferings of the Messiah and the glories that would follow. It was revealed to them that they were not serving themselves, but you, when they spoke of the things that have now been told you by those who have preached the gospel to you by the Holy Spirit sent from heaven. Even Angels long to look into these things (1 Peter 1:10-12).

Everything that was done to Jesus was predicted by the prophets in the Old Testament. At times, they even spoke in the first person, as if it happened to them. Because you will not abandon me to the realm of the dead, nor will you let your faithful one see decay (Psalm 16:10). This is spoken by David about Jesus.

Isaiah 50:5-6 gives a striking account of the shame and suffering endured by Jesus. Isaiah speaks as if these things happened to him, not Jesus. Isaiah said, "the Sovereign Lord has opened my ears; I have not been rebellious, I have not turned away. I offered my back to those who beat me, my cheeks to those who pulled out my beard; I did not hide my face from mocking and spitting. Because the Sovereign Lord helps me, I will not be disgraced. Therefore have I set my face like flint, and I know I will not be put to shame."

Isaiah 52:13-15, See, my servant will act wisely; He will be raised and lifted up and highly exalted. Just as there were many who were appalled at Him- His appearance was so disfigured beyond that of any human being and His form marred beyond human likeness- so He will sprinkle many nations, and kings will shut their mouths because of Him. For what they were not told, they will see, and what they have not heard, they will understand. He's speaking of Jesus on the cross.

I love the Scriptures in Isaiah because they paint a different picture than what is written in the New Testament. They give more detail about how disfigured Jesus' human form was on the cross. Can you imagine the pain and anguish Jesus endured having the hair pulled from His beard? His appearance being described as so disfigured beyond that of any human being and His form marred beyond human likeness? His body was basically unrecognizable! He went through all of that for me and you. He paid it all!

Then the governor's soldiers took Jesus into the Praetorium and gathered the whole company of soldiers around Him. They stripped Him and put a scarlet robe on Him, and then twisted together a crown of thorns and set it on His head. They put a staff in His right hand. Then they knelt in front of Him and mocked Him. "Hail, king of the Jews!" they said. They spit on Him and took the staff and struck Him on the head again and again. After they had mocked him, they took off the robe and put His own clothes on Him. Then they led Him away to crucify Him (Matthew 27:27-31). Micah 5:1 says they will strike the judge of Israel with a rod on the cheek. Another Old Testament prophecy about Jesus' crucifixion.

Matthew 27:35—then they crucified Him, and divided His garments, casting lots, that it may be fulfilled which was spoken by the prophet: they divided My garments among them, and for My clothing they cast lots. The prophet that says this is David in Psalm 22:18 "they divide my clothes among them and cast lots for my garment." This never happened to David, but to Jesus. This was spoken by the Holy Spirit. It's interesting to me to see how the Old and New Testament correlates. Jesus' last words from the cross are found in a Psalm by David- Psalm 22:1, "My God, my God, why have you forsaken me?"

John 19:34—Instead, one of the soldiers pierced Jesus' side with a spear, bringing a sudden flow of blood and water. I believe that this shedding of blood by Jesus is significant. Leviticus 17:11 says blood is shed for atonement (forgiveness) of sins. In fact, the law requires that nearly everything be cleansed with blood, and without the shedding of blood there is no forgiveness (Hebrews 9:22).

In the Old Testament, a lamb would be sacrificed by the high priest to atone for sins. Leviticus chapter 4 gives in detail how a lamb is to be sacrificed. In this way the priest will make atonement for them for the sin they have committed, and they will be forgiven. Jesus is our High Priest and sacrificial lamb. Upon seeing Jesus, John the Baptist proclaimed, "Look! The Lamb of God who takes away the sin of the world! (John 1:29). The prophet Isaiah wrote: "He was oppressed and He was afflicted, yet He did not open His mouth; He was led like a lamb to the slaughter, and as a sheep before it's shearer's are silent, so He opened not His mouth (Isaiah 53:7).

He was despised and rejected by mankind, a man of suffering, and familiar with pain. Like one from whom people hide their faces He was despised, and we held Him in low esteem. Surely, He took up our pain and bore our suffering, yet we considered Him punished by God, stricken by Him, and afflicted. But He was pierced for our transgressions, He was crushed for our iniquities; the punishment that brought us peace was on Him, and by His wounds we are healed. We are, like sheep, have gone astray, each of us has turned to our own way; and the Lord has laid on Him the iniquity of us all (Isaiah 53:3-6). For by one sacrifice He has made perfect forever those who are being made holy (Hebrews 10:14). Then he adds: "Their sins and lawless acts I will remember no more." And where these have been forgiven, sacrifice for sin is no longer necessary (Hebrews 10:17-18).

Therefore, there is now no condemnation for those who are in Christ Jesus, because through Christ Jesus the law of the Spirit who gives life has set you free from the law of sin and death. For what the law was powerless to do because it was weakened by the flesh, God did by sending His own Son in the likeness of sinful flesh to be a sin offering. And so He condemned sin in the flesh in order that the righteous requirement of the law might be fully met in us, who do not live according to the flesh, but according to the Spirit (Romans 8: 1-4).

God made Him who had no sin to be sin for us, so that in Him we might become the righteousness of God (2 Corinthians 5:21). Derek Prince said it best in one of his sermons. He said, "all of the evil due to us came upon Jesus that all of the good due to Him might be offered to you and me."

In Him we have redemption through His blood, the forgiveness of sins, in accordance with the riches of God's grace (Ephesians 1:7). Redeem means to buy back. Psalms 107:2—Let the redeemed of the Lord say so. I am redeemed! I am not worthy of this gift but I thank you Jesus for the sacrifice! Let go of the shame, guilt, and rejection because Jesus endured it all for us!

Chapter 13

DUST TO DUST

We have all had our loved ones die. It is very painful, and depending on who you've lost, you may feel like you don't want to live anymore. My mother died when I was nine years old. I'm not sure if it was because of that, or something else that I may have suppressed, but I used to have a fear of dying. I searched the Scriptures intently for answers about dying especially when loving, good hearted people died. I couldn't understand it!

Some of the nicest, most generous, loving people I know have died. Friends and family members who would give their last to you. When my friend Jacque died, I was heartbroken. I truly felt that people saw Jesus when they saw her. She would pray with you, encourage you, try to uplift your spirits, and was a clown! You could not be around her and have a bad day! I never heard a judging word from her lips.

The same with others like my nephew Shannon, he was such a positive person, a God fearing man. So when they died I cried out to the Lord saying, "I don't understand! There are so many mean people who don't go to church, don't believe in You, yet they're still here." God led me to read Matthew 22: 36-40—"Teacher, which is the greatest commandment in the Law?" Jesus replied: "Love the Lord your God with all your heart and with all your soul and with all your mind." This is the first and greatest commandment. And the second is like it: "Love your neighbor as yourself. All the Law and the Prophets hang on these two commandments."

These loving people that died, no doubt loved God with all of their heart, soul, and mind. They definitely loved their neighbor as themselves. I read that scripture over. If loving God and loving others is the FIRST AND GREATEST COMMANDMENT—they accomplished this! In my mind I feel like—"they had nothing else on this earth to prove."

I'm excited to know that I will see all of my family and friends again. No doubt Daddy Joe said prayers for me when I married Vincent. I wasn't the ideal wife at times, back in the day. What a laugh we will have when I see him again, discussing me writing A BOOK FULL OF SCRIPTURES!

How long are we to live?

Only God knows. Job 14:5 says a person's days are determined; You have decreed the number of his months and have set limits he cannot exceed.

Psalms 90:10 says our days may come to seventy years, or eighty, if our strength endures; yet the best of them are but trouble and sorrow, for they quickly pass, and we fly away.

James 4:14, Why, you do not even know what will happen tomorrow. What is your life? You are a mist that appears for a little while and then vanishes.

A few scriptures on how to prolong your life can be found in Exodus 20:12 Honor your father and your mother, so that you may live long in the land the Lord your God is giving you.

Proverbs 10:27 the fear of the Lord adds length to life, but the years of the wicked are cut short.

Spirit, Soul, and Body

God is a triune Being (Trinity). Three equal persons form the Godhead- The Father, The Son, and The Holy Spirit. Then God said, "Let US make mankind in our image, in our likeness, so that they may rule over the fish in the sea and the birds in the sky, over the livestock and all the wild animals, and over all the creatures that move along the ground" (Genesis 2:26).

Then the Lord God formed a man from the dust of the ground and breathed into his nostrils the breath of life, and the man became a living being (Genesis 2:7). God created a triune man- we have a spirit, soul, and body. Paul says in 1 Thessalonians 5:23—May God Himself, the God of peace, sanctify you through and through. May your whole spirit, soul and body be kept blameless at the coming of our Lord Jesus Christ.

The spirit part of us is God conscious. It is God breathed spirit from above. It is the only way to connect to God. When God told Adam that if he ate from the tree of life that he would die, he didn't mean physically die. Adam died spiritually after eating from the tree of life. He lost his connection to God. Our soul is self conscious, our emotions, our will. Our body is world conscious; physical, the senses; it is from the dirt and will return to the dirt.

I strive daily to be led by the spirit, but it is hard because the soul is about self. "I want," "I feel," "I need." Sometimes the spirit may lead you to get up and read the Bible, but your soul will say "I'll do that later, I don't feel like getting up right now." It gives new meaning to Psalms 103:1 when David says- "Praise the Lord, oh my soul, and all that is within me, praise His holy name!" It's like he's telling his soul to wake up! Praise the Lord!

After Jesus left his disciples and went away to pray, He came back and found them asleep. He said to His disciples, "Watch and pray so that you will not fall into temptation. The Spirit is willing, but the flesh is weak" (Matthew 26:41).

For only in Christ is the Spirit reconciled and reconnected. Colossians 1:21-22 says once you were alienated from God and were enemies in your minds because of your evil behavior. But now He has reconciled you by Christ's physical body, through death, to present you holy in His sight, without blemish and free from accusation.

Here are a few verses about the spirit returning to God after death. On the cross Jesus called out with a loud voice, "Father into your hands I commit my spirit." When He had said this, He breathed his last (Luke 23:46). Then in Acts 7:59—While they were stoning him, Stephen prayed, "Lord Jesus, receive my spirit."

Resurrection

Resurrection means the rising of the dead from the grave. It is our body that dies, is buried, and is resurrected NOT THE SPIRIT OR SOUL. The body is returned to the dust from which God formed it in the beginning. Our spirit returns to God. Ecclesiastes 12:7 says, and the dust returns to the ground it came from, and the spirit returns to God who gave it.

Death is not the end. The ultimate goal is for Jesus to return and for the resurrection of the body. Salvation is not complete until the body is resurrected. The body will be rejoined with spirit and we will then have an incorruptible (not subject to corruption or decay) and an immortal (not subject to dying) body like Jesus. For as in Adam all die, so in Christ all will be made alive (1 Corinthians 15:22).

Paul said that resurrection from the dead was his goal. He said, "I want to know Christ- yes, to know the power of His resurrection and participation in His sufferings, becoming like Him in His death, and so, somehow, attaining to the resurrection from the dead (Philippians 3:10-11). He said, "I press on toward the goal to win the prize for which God has called me heavenward in Christ Jesus" (v.14). In Romans he said that we wait eagerly for our adoption to sonship, the redemption of our bodies (Romans 8:23).

Brothers and sisters, we do not want you to be uninformed about those who sleep in death, so that you do not grieve like the rest of mankind, who have no hope. For we believe that Jesus died and rose again, and so we believe that God will bring with Jesus those who have fallen asleep in Him. According to the Lord's Word, we tell you that we who are still alive who are left until the coming of the Lord, will certainly not precede those who have fallen asleep. For the Lord Himself will come down from heaven, with a loud command of the archangel and with the trumpet call of God, and the dead in Christ will rise first. After that, we who are still alive and are left will be caught up together with them in the clouds to meet the Lord in the air. And so, we will be with the Lord forever (1 Thessalonians 4:13-17).

Multitudes who sleep in the dust of the earth will awake, some to everlasting life, others to shame and everlasting contempt (Daniel 12:3).

Matthew 24:36-42—But about that day or hour no one knows, not even the angels in heaven, nor the Son, but only the Father. As it was in the days of Noah, so it will be at the coming of the Son of Man. For in the days before the flood, people were eating and drinking, marrying and giving in marriage, up to the day Noah entered the ark; and they knew nothing about what would happen until the flood came and took them all away. That is how it will be at the coming of the son of man. Two men will be in the field; one will be taken and the other left. Two women will be grinding with the hand mill; one will be taken and the other left. Therefore, keep watch, because you do not know on what day your Lord will come.

Our body will reunite with our spirit. 1 Corinthians 15:42-49 says describes the changes we will see. So will it be with the resurrection of the dead. The body that is sown is perishable, it is raised imperishable; it is sown in dishonor, it is raised in glory; it is sown in weakness, it is raised in power; it is a natural body, it is raised a spiritual body. If there is a natural body, there is also a spiritual body. (v. 49)—just as we have borne the image of the earthly man, so shall we bear the image of the heavenly man. Currently our soul makes decisions, but after resurrection our spirits will control us.

For Christ also suffered once for sins, the righteous for the unrighteous, to bring you to God. He was put to death in the body but made alive in the Spirit (1 Peter 3:18). And just as it is appointed for man to die once, and after that comes judgement (Hebrews 9:27). For the wages of sin is death, but the free gift of God is eternal life in Christ Jesus our Lord (Romans 6:23).

Will we see our loved ones again?

To answer this question let's look at one passage. A story told by Jesus in Luke 16:19-31.

There was a rich man who was dressed in purple and fine linen and lived in luxury every day. At his gate was laid a beggar named Lazarus, covered with sores and longing to eat what fell from the rich man's table. Even the dogs came and licked his sores.

The time came when the beggar died and the Angels carried him to Abraham's side. The rich man also died and was buried. In Hades, where he was in torment, he looked up and saw Abraham far away, with Lazarus by his side. So he called to him, "Father Abraham, have pity on me and send Lazarus to dip the tip of his finger in water and cool my tongue, because I am in agony in this fire."

But Abraham replied, "Son, remember that in your lifetime you received your good things, while Lazarus received bad things, but now he is comforted here and you are in agony. And besides all this, between us and you a great chasm has been set in place, so that those who want to go from here to you cannot, nor can anyone crossover from there to us."

He answered, "Then I beg you, father, send Lazarus to my family, for I have five brothers. Let him warn them, so that they will not also come to this place of torment." Abraham replied, "They have Moses and the Prophets; Let them listen to them." "No Father Abraham," he said, "but if someone from the dead goes to them, they will repent." He said to him, "If they do not listen to Moses and the Prophets, they will not be convinced even if someone rises from the dead."I think that this being told by Jesus helps us to see what to expect after the resurrection, which is good news for those of us who have family and friends who have gone on before us. We can see that the rich man still recognized Lazarus, so identity wasn't lost. The rich man remembered that he had five brothers on earth, so memory wasn't lost. The rich man recognized that he was being tormented in fire, so he was aware of his present condition. But what I found the most disheartening was that the chasm that separated them. He was able to recognize that there was complete separation between them that couldn't be crossed. God, I pray that I never witness this!

Another thing that I found interesting was Father Abraham's last sentence when he said, "If they don't listen to Moses and the Prophets, they will not be convinced even if someone rises from the dead." How true this statement is! Jesus rose from the dead, yet we still have people who aren't convinced!

When you truly understand death, dying and the resurrection there's no need to fear death. Philippians 1:21 Paul said, for me to live is Christ and to die is gain. I don't think Paul was saying he was ready to die. I think Paul understood that death meant he would be in the presence of the Lord. In 2 Corinthians 5:8, he says, "we are confident, I say, and would prefer to be away from the body and at home with the Lord." Or as I like to say "absent from the body, is present with the Lord."

We shall be with the Lord and be with one another for eternity. Jesus is coming back to claim those who belong to Him (1 Corinthians 15:23). He has a Book of Life. Only those written in the Book of Life will be resurrected. And if someone's name was not found written in the Book of Life, he was thrown into the lake of fire (Revelations 20:15). Unless you repent, you too will perish (Luke 13:3). For we must all appear before the judgment seat of Christ, so that each of us may receive what is due us for the things done while in the body, whether good or bad (2 Corinthians 5:10). We all will see Jesus on that day because He is both Savior and the Judge. For the Father judges no one but has given all judgement to the Son (John 5:22). This will take place on the day when God judges people's secrets through Jesus Christ, as my gospel declares (Romans 2:16). "And He has given Him authority to judge because He is the Son of Man" (John 5:27).

What a tragedy for the ones who do not know Christ. For God so loved the world that He gave his one and only Son, that whoever believes in Him shall not perish but have eternal life. For God did not send His Son into the world to condemn the world, but to save the world through Him. Whoever believes in Him is not condemned, but whoever does not believe stands condemned already because they have not believed in the name of God's one and only Son (John 3:16-18).

Therefore God exalted Him to the highest place and gave Him the name that is above every name, that at the name of Jesus every knee should bow, in heaven and on earth, and under the earth, and every tongue acknowledge that Jesus Christ is Lord, to the glory of God the Father. (Philippians 2:9-10). The time has come. The kingdom of God has come near. Repent and believe the good news! (Mark 1:15).

Not sure where you will spend eternity?

Romans 10:9 says that if you confess with your mouth, "Jesus is Lord," and believe in your heart that God raised him from the dead, you will be saved. For it is with your heart that you believe and are justified, and it is with your mouth that you profess your faith and are saved. Verse 13—for "Everyone who calls on the name of the Lord will be saved."

Prayer for Salvation

I tell you, now is the time of God's favor, now is the day of salvation (2 Corinthians 6:2). Jesus answered, "I am the way and the truth and the life. No one comes to the Father except through Me" (John 14:6).

Say this prayer out loud and receive the free gift of salvation:

Lord Jesus, I believe that you are the Son of God,

That You died on the cross for my sins, was buried,

and rose from the dead.

I repent of my sins and ask for Your forgiveness.

Come into my life and be my personal Lord and Savior.

In Jesus' name,

Amen.